Small Boat, Big Sea

PETER OWEN JONES is rector of three parishes near Cambridge. His experiences at theological college are described in his first book *Bed of Nails*. He also gained some notoriety when in 1996 he gave a blessing for the protesters at the Newbury bypass. He lives with his wife and four children.

For India, Jonson,
Harris and Eden

SMALL BOAT BIG SEA

One

year's

journey

as a

parish

priest

Peter Owen Jones

LION

Published by
Lion Publishing plc
Wilkinson House, Jordan Hill Road, Oxford, OX2 8DR, England
www.lionhudson.com
ISBN 0 7459 5053 1

First hardback edition 2000
First paperback edition 2001
10 9 8 7 6 5 4 3 2 1 0

A catalogue record for this book is available
from the British Library

Typeset in 11/15 Garamond

Preface

You have to be a fool to describe the stars, a fool or drunk. A bank of trees or a rookery or a bench scrawled with ridiculous love and yesterday's scores – look at it, set beneath the leaves on the edge of some public cricket pitch, or stuck against the fence as children throw themselves around in the playground, the place where you sit and smoke, admire the litter, maybe. But the stars: they have defeated the poets. Maybe I am asking an embryo to describe their mother's face.

After theological college we went to the Fens. You either love the Fens or hate them. I hated the fact that they would end, that when you hit Cambridge you were back in normality, the ordinariness of factories and fashion.

As a priest you almost have to give up belonging. I didn't understand this at all; if anything I assumed that the church was some sort of cosseted comfort zone. It is quite the opposite, I'm pleased to say. You become a traveller. That's no big deal really; it may be a more honest appraisal of who we are and what we are. Permanence is an illusion for those who cannot bear the thought of their own death, their rotting flesh and horrific features. Don't worry about it: enjoy it.

I thought being a priest was about permanence. I was wrong. It is about reconciling the impermanence of humanity to the permanence of God. As a Christian, as a priest, you have to take sacrifice on board. The theory that love is umbilically linked to sacrifice, demonstrated on the cross of

Jesus Christ, makes lovely poetry, spills tears – but to be tied to it, however reluctantly, tests and tears. You soon learn the absolute emptiness of those who are prepared to give what has cost them nothing. Real love is expensive. So it should be; it demands a part of you. That is its cost.

The lessons of theological college were all very sweet but putting them into practice demands more than most of us can give. To that extent we are always in debt to a God who does nothing other than give.

As a priest, as a Christian, you have to carry Christianity. You are an official representative, and Christianity is judged by your capacity for it. I wrote this book in the second year of being in some parishes on my own, and I stand by what I have written. Reading it, you might think, All this bloke does is swan around on mountains, visit Europe and rant. It may seem that way. But I have to say that it was only possible to write down five per cent of what happens on a daily basis. The rest is private, and it is critical that it remains that way. So much of what a priest does is confidential; you are a keeper of fears, hopes, faults, tears. If people are brave enough to show you their soul then they expect you to keep it in a safe place. It was also a strange year in that we went away more in one year than we had done in the previous ten, which was down to the generosity of the Friends of the Clergy Corporation, my late father-in-law's will and some long-suffering friends. I can't say that I wrote the book for money. I wrote it because I wanted to.

The main tensions arise between belonging to God and belonging to an institution that represents this God. It is at this point that you are left trying to manhandle light into light bulbs. Some people can do it. The Church of England is sleeping, covered in dust, warmed by the enchantment of time. Its traditions are slowly filling its lungs, drowning substance. It has cold blood, curdled in a cautious conservatism that has

Preface

failed to evolve and, over the years, steadily atrophies most of
what it touches; this has largely been down to the way it sees
itself – its self-image, and those who have bought into it.
I'm not sure the Church of England has a defined sense of self
anymore. It was clearly more self-assured in the past. You can
feel that, between the lines of old theology. It's rich with self-
assurance, accepting a role carved by the state and polished by
the public – if there ever was such a time. Some people cling
to that, want the dust and the worn pages of used books. I love
it too; in some ways it is what makes the church distinctive
from the rest of society. It needs to be distinctive, but we can't
hang on to what *made* it distinctive, call it tradition and leave
it at that. It is the very nature of those traditions, which were
there to help people understand what it was to be a Christian,
that have somehow consumed us, consumed our faith.

Christ, it would appear, did not spend hours and hours
discussing the historical significance of the wise men, the
virgin birth, homosexuality. Is that the legacy he intended?
While I recognise this is, in part, down to the long and bloody
debate over authority, God's authority and where that comes
from, I'm afraid I do not share the view that scripture is the
single point on which this authority spins. I can see no reason
in a multi-sense world for God to choose but one line of
authoritative revelation. I consider the sky, the degradation of
war, drops of paint, the dew, on and on: all this is revelation.
I am more concerned that those claiming authority from
scripture obviously have some need of it.

The debate over language, liturgy, raises huge passions. The
colour of my stole on any particular Sunday, celebrating the
saints, preaching the word, the original Greek, the original
Latin, consecrated ground, unconsecrated ground, the
hymns on Mothering Sunday, family services, faculties, taking
communion, wearing a hat, not wearing a hat… Is it the lilies

that belong to God, or the lack of them in Lent? All this and too much more has become Christianity, has somehow come to symbolise it, come to be what makes it distinctive, because it all seems terribly important to us. If that is the sum of it, perceived or otherwise, then it is hardly surprising we stand where we do. Whether you like it or not, that is what has made us distinctive; it is our failing to have hung on to it all.

I have to ask why we are where we are; so may you. You could say the church has not bowed down to the modern world; you would be right, absolutely, although I remain confused about whether this has been a conscious decision or a complete accident. A complete accident would appear to make more sense, having seen the way it has been run. It is still running away, still cannot face the modern world, perhaps because it will see its reflection in it.

In theology college we were force-fed Christ, and maybe that ultimately is the point of it all; none of the rest of it really mattered. There was a lot of other stuff as well that was useful, but I'm not sure that, at the end of the day, it made a difference. You see we were not taught to communicate; we were taught what Christ communicates. That may appear to leave us several pieces short of the contemporary jigsaw, but Providence surely belongs to God.

I will not write any more diaries like this, not until I make it to the road, should I be so lucky.

I would like to thank everyone who lives in Haslingfield, Harlton, and Great and Little Eversden for making this book possible; Maurice Lyon, Bill Neil-Hall, Jeff Watson and Jim Rhone for their support; Marcia Stephens for typing it; the Queen's Head in Newton and the Morpeth Arms; The Clash and the cathedrals on Radio Three's live broadcasts of afternoon services for their inspirational music; and my beautiful wife and our children for spending evenings alone while this was written.

September

It's September. Autumn has come early, it seems, blowing the death wind. East Anglia has these thick white skies that creep in off the North Sea, licking the leaves, clinging to the brambles, their thorns dripping without rain.

I serve four churches in different parishes. Haslingfield is a large barn of a place: the spiders have got the better of the corners, the lead in all the windows has bowed, and the glass in the endless diamond panes is dulled by the chalk which runs down off the clunch walls. The corners at the back are untidy with scratched gas bottles, boxes of books, chipped vases, which invariably were given away; they were too pale to keep. It is tired and there is not enough light. Harlton is a jewel. It's set back from the road behind a green glebe; inside is an ultimate space which God always enlarges. The rooks in the spring make more noise than we do, the sun charges in through the south windows sometimes and sits with us. There are two churches in the Eversdens, one tucked away in a farmyard, the other, which is locked onto a bend, is surrounded by tall chestnut trees on the edge of an immense field that stretches to the top of the hill rising to the south. It is cracked badly and the peacock butterflies which cocoon themselves under the eaves fly up and down the aisles when it gets warm enough in the spring. Last year I took thirty-eight of them off the east window and let them go outside in handfuls. I don't get to the Eversdens much; a retired priest comes and takes the Sunday services. He has the most incredible skin, smooth, hardly a wrinkle on it at all, and eyes made from candlelight.

Today I was in London. The subject was marriage, we'd spoken on the phone. I should have known the script was already written. They wanted certain answers, they needed to know the worst. They sat me down behind a desk. Behind that they had spread a piece of black cloth on the windowsill and on that they had placed a small wooden cross. So this was the church – the sombre scene was set, pre-conceived in a gothic womb, holding on in a garret somewhere, nowhere, only receiving a black and white signal. The gem in my pocket did not come out. How you had to tell the bride to hitch up her dress when she knelt down for the blessing, otherwise she was liable to wrench the front of her dress off – it has happened I'm told, and her breasts come tumbling out – that is what they wanted. In the end we talked about stress, the stress of getting married. The interviewer was in full cry, he was high on punch-ups in the pews, families falling out over napkins, fathers not talking to sons. They were determined to daub us in disbelief with the details of the ex-lover who burst into the church and objected to the marriage of her old boyfriend. This is entertainment, prime time, taking seven million of us up the aisle at once. Cameras are so quiet, they never say no. It's easy to relax, lovely to feel that people are listening to what you say and that it matters. They had the perfect title too: 'Weddings from Hell'. I made the mistake of trying to be light, funny, but it was obvious they were not interested. They wanted the juicy bits, nerves, sweat. I gave them sweat.

The bit about always bursting into tears, they cut that. It's always incredibly moving to stand there in front of two people and hear them say those beautiful words. It usually reduces me to tears. It actually becomes more incredible the more you do it. It is never ordinary. Those sentences are not well worn on any of us; we usually only say them once, they are new every time they are spoken. They are the pathway between one life and another. To stand there two feet away is an immense privilege. It is impossible to be a voyeur. You become part of it, part of that hope, part of that belief, part of all that glorious innocence. Does the video remind you how you felt? No one can see that, can they? Our feelings have become big business, especially our extreme feelings. The lie is that real life is like this, that it revolves around the gory bits. Dennis Potter's swan song was interesting last night, the final act in his final play as the main character hitting us with those bits of our life that flash before us, or so they say, just before we die. They might have been extraordinary fifty years ago, but out of context you just need to jam a logo on the end of this thirty-second sequence and it becomes a commercial. The media replay our extremes and entertain us with other people's. Have you ever thought just how much of your time you're giving them? How many hours a week are lost in newspapers, immersed in magazines, how much of your journey is lit by the radio? Film directors do an even better job on us. Look at the brilliance of Steven Spielberg – you remember when the space ship comes out of the sky in *Close Encounters*? The soldiers lying on the D-Day sand in *Saving Private Ryan*, the mayhem of wasted life contorted as it falls, fails? ET taking off in the bicycle basket? You were never there, you were never there.

There was a wedding today, a Christian and a Muslim. The sun came out just before the bride arrived in this huge blue car that matched the colours of the bridesmaids' satin. No matter where you get married in the Home Counties it seems there is always one kilt. Or maybe there is just one bloke who rents himself out plus kilt. The bloke in the kilt today was in charge of the sound system, he was there in the aisles armed with the remote control unit. I was outside when the bride arrived. By the time we opened the door the music was still going – just. As the bride started walking it stopped completely, so she was led down on the arm of her father in total silence. It was as if everyone was holding their breath. The raging pink and purple saris were also shocking, they embarrassed the brown Church of England pews. Church pews have a brown all of their own; there is nothing particularly joyful about it, they are usually the colour of gravy. They all tend to have the feeling of public transport about them. Maybe they work in small churches; in large churches they just add to the feeling of brown. There was an article in the *Church Times* this week saying that the lighting in churches was, by and large, worse than an east European bus garage. That is true; we haven't invested in it. But is it a necessity or a luxury? The first thing one of the female wedding guests today asked for was the loo, understandable really after an hour and a half's drive. There is no charming way of saying we don't have one. You may just get away with pointing towards the bushes if it is a man under fifty asking the question. You may even get a laugh out of it. It is patently not funny if you are a woman. Most rural churches don't actually have the sanitation of an east European bus garage. What annoys me is that Parochial Church Councils or PCCs have had eighty years or so to actually put them in and in far too many cases most of them have somehow come up with an argument against doing so. It is the same argument for keeping uncomfortable gravy-coloured pews. I didn't tell the young woman that we were waiting to hear from English Heritage about our £300,000 grant application to bring the two pieces of our tower back together again. Maybe in the circumstances she would have found that quite amusing. None of this spoiled the wedding; it was wonderful.

It is the first of five harvest festivals tomorrow.

There was a blue tit in Harlton Church, banging the windows. Someone had stood sunflowers in the porch on end up against the columns; they sang the loudest. I arrived with five minutes to go and handed out the service sheets. Haslingfield had been pretty fraught. The racket at the back of the church has to be healthy; all ages of children, all talking at once, which is fine. It just means that we carry on as normal. The pomp is reduced by the circumstances. The numinous sense of God held at the centre of our souls, the part we are in fact sure of, the point where something happens, this is the God we crave. The one everyone finds so hard to believe in, this God who does not use words like we do; you simply become acutely aware of the unspoken. This unspoken language is something we, all of us, are fluent in. You perhaps have to be a child or prepared to become a child to hear it, to believe it, to acknowledge the point where something happens, the point where time is made timeless. That takes peace maybe, or maybe we just think it does. To look for God is one thing, to expect God to turn up on cue is another. The traditional prompt is silence, so that we are not distracted – the theory goes – so that we can focus our minds, our souls on this search, on this sense. Surely it is an awareness, nothing else.

We have over time it seems, though, succumbed to a mixture of methodologies which masquerade as tradition. We have made worship sacred at the expense of God; have become content to give him silver, not our souls, as we slip in and out of various degrees of noise and silence. We are worshipping the manual. The Church of England has forgotten England; we are lost in the realms of Pictavia, stuttering Rome, drowning in ink. We have not embraced England for fear of offending God and ending up with safety pins in our ears. We have become stone, organs, bells, theology, cassocks and history. Church has become chalice, 'He took the cup.' We have learned how to extract God from this order, from this silence, even while we learn what to expect. But if we have a God singing to us every second there is always hope that the children hear him better: Come down from behind your high altar with your wafers and your wine and your words, come and talk to me, come and sit with me. The children had the day. I spilt all the wafers, Tony helped me pick them up and off he went to the back; we were released.

We spent a couple of weeks down in Devon in the summer. I heard about this priest in Clovelly. He used to go down to the quay, turn a lobster pot upside down and use it as an altar. Why have we privatised altars in churches? Why have we stuck them there and told everybody that they cannot move? Surely they are everywhere: a bench in Soho Square, a rock on Scaféll, a bus stop. These could all be altars; we perhaps don't see them that way, that's all.

I've forgotten Monday completely. It's Friday now; it's supposed to be a day off. The school piled into church for 'their' harvest festival this morning. This was a joint venture between the Methodist minister and myself; we have to be seen holding hands. We started off with the theme tune to *Star Wars* and then set about Genesis chapter 1. We couldn't sing any hymns because the children don't know any. That's not such a great loss when it comes to 'All Things Bright and Beautiful', which really should have been filed at the back of the cupboard a long time ago, along with 'Onward Christian Soldiers' and a few others.

The humanists have filled the gap with their 'songs for assemblies'; most of these don't actually mention the G word at all. The compositions are very big on manners. We sang about harvest – 'It's Harvest Time, It's Harvest Time Again' – but the 'berries on the trees and big bumble bees' were free agents. This was creation without a creator. It just happened to be; there was no poet. We stared at the cells without wonder.

Do you think adults feel as out of place singing children's songs as children feel singing supposedly adult hymns? The children fidgeted fantastically in the front under Haslingfield's serious ceiling.

Thursday was a fourteen-hour day. Somewhere in the middle there was a sandwich; there was a PCC meeting in the evening, we were talking toilets again. The church is crumbling. It's made from clunch, most of the churches around here are. It was the local stone dug out about half a mile from where the church stands in Haslingfield. It's very beautiful actually, a rich creamy grey, not sombre at all. On the inside, past wisdom was to whitewash the whole lot. This is now peeling which leaves you feeling like you're entombed on the inside of a cheese grater. Anyway the beautiful church held up moderately well over the centuries until acid rain. Acid rain on clunch, which is compressed chalk, has much the same effect as water on an Alka-Seltzer tablet – the building is literally dissolving. After a lot of discussion we are going to ask three architects to come up with suggestions as to where loos and meeting rooms and a small kitchen area should go. Some people want them inside, some people want them outside. I hope this won't dissolve into another Westminster – the choirmaster and the dean – but believe you me this is a result indeed: at least most of us agree we need them.

I was invited to address the Retired Clergy Association today in a church in Cambridge. It was all very organised, lots of new paint and some loos upstairs, no mirrors. The subject was Woodland Burial. This seems to have caused quite a stir as half of the twenty-four who were attending didn't manage to fall asleep during my presentation. Apparently it's usual for most of them to nod off. It must be an incredibly surreal experience, addressing a roomful of people who've all fallen asleep. It's sure to happen sometime.

Cambridge is jammed with churches – I don't know how many there are. They all have their own traditions. All the colleges have chapels as well. This is senseless really, having a fundamentalist Evangelical church, an Anglo-Catholic establishment and many more. Why? One or two should do it surely, and the resources should be spread more evenly among the rest of the church. It's about upholding tradition again; even worse, the particular tradition of a particular church. What tradition did they have before they were saddled with the one they have now? Our city-centre churches are surely the ones that should be doing city-centre things: meeting people in art and music, feeding the hungry. There must be about eight churches in a geographical area equivalent to the village in which I live, all competing with each other, all offering the same thing in slightly different colours: insanity. This addiction to tradition makes junkies. That's how it survives, not only by defining God but by imposing that definition as truth and, even worse, as reality. We are in danger of selling love for certainty. Why have we become so obsessed with church? It's all very one-dimensional, this focus on Sundays. Everyone knows the story pretty much, so why do we keep telling it? Shouldn't we be offering ourselves as a sacrifice? Our blood has become thin.

The trouble is, the way things are at the moment you are

either in or you are out. We tout our version of events and the meaning of life, and if people happen not to agree with this we call them atheists and condemn them to suffering. I don't want to make excuses for people in coffins who never went to church, or read some of those ridiculous words in the funeral service that are so exclusive to Christian belief that ninety per cent of the people who have died felt unable to express that belief. God cannot love me any more or any less than he loves you. My life aches with sin; it is made even more real by the fact that I believe 100 per cent in God. The ardent atheist Richard Dawkins would doubtless say I am a fool. I am, but not for the reasons Mr Dawkins would give you. When we both meet with this God we will have been fools for totally different reasons. Mr Dawkins for quite rightly refusing to be condemned to heaven, and me for abusing it. I'm off to Durham tomorrow: the conference on apologetics and the mass media.

The Dutchman was quite brilliant, Dr Albert van de Heuval. We had the regulation theological supper, carrots and something else. He said that we shouldn't moan about the media, that it was a gift from God, that human beings either made it beautiful or made it ugly. There is no doubt that it is our own reflection. He tore the church to pieces. He said that of all the special interest groups no other is given so much preferential treatment by the media: the Sunday slots on television, 'Thought for the Day', the awful flower-festival calendars in local papers. He's right and the whole lot should be canned, that's what he said. Unless religious programming is subjected to the same ruthless criteria as the rest of it, the public will soon rumble the spin. They have, but maybe that's the game plan. 'Songs of Praise' is a charade; yes there are more people that watch it than go to church on Sunday, but is that the reality of the love of God, of Christ the man? At best it's our response to it, our ordered response to it.

Dr van de Heuval said the media was sick to the back teeth of the church complaining about it and simultaneously turning into raging luvvies the moment they were asked to appear on it. He mentioned our arrogant legacy, the church's capacity for writing its own glorious history and reporting it in nothing less than glowing terms. It's a sham, but then the media have been unwilling in the extreme to enter into any form of meaningful self-criticism, and as for rewriting history to suit the popular palate, theirs is compromised by the need to entertain. At least the church has a few rebels in its ranks who are, on the whole, tolerated as being valuable; they used to be burned. No, there are no excuses if the entertainment fails. The Church of England have found that out; the television companies are too busy going global to bother with apologetics. Maybe they are today's church: the point where we meet meaning, the world as it is and our response to it creates the rooms in which we live. That's fine if the information coming through the medium is reliable and not ultimately self-serving. The real problem is that when the truth is sacrificed or twisted for entertainment you ultimately end up with comedy. It's funny the first time.

It was the Newcastle Brown that did for me. A couple of bottles of glorious Dog and all seemed sensuous. The mist was already here wrapping the cathedral in a rich Christmas. The bells are damp, cushioned in Evian air. We had the bishop this morning. The only thing that rescued the sermon was that he rushed headlong into every hole that had been dug the night before by Dr van de Heuval. Here was the inherent suspicion of all things sensational and the inherent mistrust of the media moguls who come to us baring breasts. After that we were bundled into four groups to present the case for and against a hot topic. This was all to be done in front of the cameras which had been wired up in the conference hall. Our scenario was a mystical edict from the European court that sexual relationships, as long as they were consenting, were OK at sixteen. To spice this up it was also to be an offence under European law to disclose the details of someone else's sex life. This was doubtless inspired by President Clinton's remark last week that he felt his private life had been criminalised, which sounds like he's trying to blame everyone else for his own actions. He'll probably get away with it as well.

You can't really legislate against sex at sixteen. John Peel, the disc jockey, said that our early adventures into music were signs of the first steps into adulthood and that they were largely free from parental control. Parents can apply pressure, which usually goes along the lines of 'Will you turn that awful racket down!' which for most adolescents must just add to the pure delight of it all. That first taste, can you remember it? the first piece of music that was yours, that meant something to you. The one that opened your young soul. To offer the alternative of no sex before marriage is fine, to give people the choice of celibacy until marriage; can this teach the soul the value of love? Marriage is the cauldron of love, the place where we actually learn to love once we have recovered from falling in love. Surely we are all looking for the freedom of intimacy that only love can really give us. Most of my generation fell in love with a body, with a face; we weren't looking for the soul, we were looking for sex. There was a woman once who told me that to fall in love over forty, as she had done, was the most powerful experience of her life. We have perhaps forgotten how to fall in love; falling into bed hasn't helped us. We're all told it's freedom, freedom to express our sexual selves and how important that is. This woman fell in love and although she had married before and although she said, 'I repeated "I love you" to five different people before that point,' she said she felt bereft of the language, the vocabulary of love. Surely Christ's indictment of divorce and adultery is not a hard disciplinarian line. It is there firstly to say that this language above all else is sacred, that love is sacred, that marriage is sacred. You will not learn it if you are distracted by sex. You will learn it by looking for it, by taking it seriously. It is the point where we touch the purpose and heart of God. In giving, in sacrifice, in joy, these are constituents of love. The temptation is to ignore the whole lot, get pissed, pout and pull. This may temporarily solve our crisis of loneliness, but the end effect is surely to make us more lonely.

The church has conclusively failed in imposing its sexual ethics on this generation. Thankfully its authority is shot to pieces on this issue and so it should be – standing on the edges in the fields of teenage love offering echoes of lines that damn them for what they are doing. We lost the argument a generation ago; it's about time we faced up to why that happened. Maybe then we can console ourselves by becoming more conservative than we already are, but it is essentially a remedy for our own failings, nobody else's. It's not a response to the liberal values that have so shaped our post-war society, it's a reaction to it, proof if you like that the church has not engaged with our culture at all and has cast itself in the remnant role. Yes, it would be better if we could boast about our bruises. Why do we pretend we don't have them?

We go on about protecting the vulnerable in our society. We will do this far better by teaching and offering them love, not creating in them a legacy of guilt for failing to live up to Christ's words. The legacy of the stance that the church has taken is the awful gulf that now exists between sex and love. We go on about the love of God; the fact is we've been very big on

God and far too lean on love. God and love are synonymous.
We cannot impose love, we can only offer it. Why should God
mean one thing and love another? Without love, as Paul says, I
am but a clanging gong: that is what we have become, clanging
on about this, clanging on about that. As a result, love has
become a by-product of sex, the elixir of human being richly
crippled by our own paralysing vanity.

We had Sir Bernard Ingham to supper this evening. He looked
more like a Saint Bernard who drank most of the brandy he
came into contact with. He entertained us to begin with with
a collection of his own epitaphs; he has over the years been
called a poodle, a menace to democracy, and more recently
the *Independent* heckled that he was a poisoned lump of suet.
His advice over the issue of the Spirit Zone in the Millennium
Dome was to go to Peter Mandelson and get nasty, to leave
him in no doubt that this was a Christian celebration and that
Mr Mandelson should liberate some of his seven hundred and
fifty million quid to make that point; that it was essential for
organised religion to get its message across. Religion and the
contemporary understanding of the word 'organised' have
nothing in common whatsoever. The media have wised up
to the fact that whatever a bishop says, there's more than
likely going to be another bishop that disagrees. There is no
party line. While this is incredibly liberating on an individual
basis, it is suicide in a media culture that thrives on dissent,
disagreement and sensation. We are never going to be able
to manage it; that would actually be a defeat of what we say
we believe in. We have to try to explain why we are prone to
disagreeing with each other, why we are subject to the same
ridiculous weaknesses as everybody else, why God has chosen
in his wisdom to make fools out of us and flood every single

newspaper, radio and television station with stories about our own essential weakness.

Have we not surrendered our souls for the benign assurance of freedom? Has this become an illusion created for us by those who need us to believe in it. What exactly are we free to do or choose? Free choice in this society is in danger of being boiled down to what supermarket you shop in, what car you drive, what shirt you wear, who insures the contents of your house. Is this what you have chosen or is this something that has been chosen for you? We have been subjugated; we have been consumed by consumerism, allowed to gorge on consumption without conscience, our lives increasingly defined by labels that we have foolishly allowed to speak for us. The price for playing this poisonous game is a surrender of our own identity; it is no wonder that fashion designers are heralded as gods, and models as their angels. The photographer has become the icon, the icons they produce merely extensions of their own personality. We all end up wishing we were somebody else. God becomes mean for not making you as beautiful as the mirage in the magazine. You are just as beautiful: you were made with the same care that modelled the universe. Is a daffodil more beautiful than a tulip? To wish you were like the artist, the model, the politician, the MD, actually places you in their hands. You give up a part of yourself to them. What Christianity fails to get across all the time is that God enhances, refines, enriches. The world you see with God in your eyes is free of ambition, free of envy, free of guilt actually. You are set free from the labels that force themselves upon you ultimately for their own profit; none of these matter. It doesn't mean they should burn necessarily, but to pretend that they can cover the cracks of our insecurity, to allow them to express who we are, to allow our possessions to define us completely, means we are being possessed by them.

September

We are all broken priests; we are all broken people. We have all been rescued by God; we are all completely imperfect. It's no good looking at priests and saying it was the only thing we could do and that we are essentially misfits with the social graces of a cracked cup. That is true, and it is also true of you as well. To pretend otherwise – and that's what we all try to do – is in fact the weaker option. To keep your cracks out of sight is supposedly a luxury of the so-called able-bodied, the so-called sound of mind. Maybe separation from God here on this planet is something we did choose, each of us. God surely does not want to crush us, and if we are loved unconditionally that surely has to mean that we are free to be as we are. Free to hate, free to murder, to love, to give, to feel, to cheat, to steal, to lie – especially to ourselves. A very attractive option when you are confronted with your own cracks is firstly to deny them, secondly to blame God for them and thirdly to ignore them and God completely. But the willingness of those who believe in God to entertain these cracks in their cup isn't done out of some spiritual sadomasochism. It is actually an attempt to deal with them, to live with them rather than exist in a constant state of spiritual war. In a society where the love of God has almost become a taboo, the analyst, the psychotherapist becomes the mender of cracks. People don't tend to go to church to be made whole, to realise the sense of wholeness any more, not really. We prefer medicine, Prozac and psychotherapy; counselling is such a comfortable word. We have saved God for Sundays and the sweet memory of our mother's voice singing as she held our hand, as the light rushed in through those extraordinary windows. We want that feeling and the little pieces of untidy ritual that can perhaps induce it. But God is not the universal healer any more; she is, he is seen and blamed for causing our wounds, mentioned as the Father of all suffering as science rides the horizon to save all of us from the pain of human being. Jesus is saved for the hard cases: the deranged, the socially inept, the oversensitive, and everyone who's too flimsy to play sport on Sunday mornings. We are learning to take pleasure in our pain, too; our cracks are fascinating, rich veins of feeling. Christianity at least recognises, values pain, it isn't something to numb. This is very different from the desensitising that goes on in many different masks: nicotine, booze, vanity, the delusions we allow ourselves, the excuses we make for things as they are. We can never grow unless we come face to face with why we have chosen them.

It's the last full day, the mist is still with us. Durham is a fantastic town, it lets you imagine. The trees growing down by the river are unbroken, the water is black, the gulls float in between the high banks. Opposite the college is a garden, the iron gate has a twisted chain that holds the two sides together. On the other side it is thick with azaleas, all in bloom; they are not there on weeded soil and filed in trim symmetry; all their Polaroid colours haunt the hessian air.

Durham Cathedral hangs between orange and brown. The pillars on the inside are cut deep into abstract patterns, the huge space always holding every word. The ambition they profess is enormous: here we try to demonstrate heaven. The effort required to build them must have been immense. Most of the cathedrals took over a hundred years to finish. They are still unfinished, always unfinished; maybe that's what they should be. We call the process of maintaining them upkeep. Durham needs £700,000 a year. The question is, are we splashing out here to maintain a picture of God as God used to be, or are these magnificent buildings still meaningful? We maintain the rhythms of history in them. There are services throughout the day. There must have been no more than twenty of us at evensong. Can they reflect a contemporary view of God, or are they locked in state, locked in stone to what God was? Under the current regime, undoubtedly. If they are to survive as more than museums of faith they will need new meaning.

Elaine Storkey was going at 90 mph this morning. She told a great story. She was part of a programme that had invited Jeffrey Archer onto the discussion panel. He sat in his chair for the rehearsal. Elaine, who was watching the whole thing on monitors, commented that he looked absolutely terrible – ugly and ghost-like, definitely terminally ill; his eyes were sunken and his features blown out of all proportion. The lighting cameraman turned to her and smiled. He then announced, with a degree of charm, that he had lit him that way. This is how Lord Archer looked after the treatment. Elaine finished with a story about a woman who, when asked to describe her thread-like faith, declared that when she held a shell to her ear there was Jesus in the sensation, in the sound. This was some cause for concern: Jesus as sensation was too far in evangelical terms from 'Jesus is Lord'. What exactly does that mean? 'Jesus is the light of the world': what does that mean? We trot these lines out and are confused when they don't appear to work; they are ignored because people don't understand them. Outside a Christian context they are meaningless. They are lines for the end of an advertisement, but in the absence of a decent advertisement they don't make any sense at all. The phrase 'Jesus is Lord', patched up in yellow, spoken with eyes half-closed, quoted as fact, wielded as certainty, is nothing other than uncut self-importance. In a non-Christian context it does nothing other than confirm the serial insanity of Christians. Worst of all, it takes the essence of the Christian faith and, in communication terms, renders it totally, totally meaningless. It is perceived as a defence against reality, a weapon and a prop for those who need one. It's nonsense.

The woman holding the shell to her ear expressed what Jesus feels like. Jesus is sensation, Jesus is feeling maybe, Jesus is light, Jesus is sound, Jesus is love, Jesus is seeing, Jesus is eternity, Jesus is colour, Jesus is one, Jesus is silence, Jesus is Easter, Jesus is grace, Jesus is forgiveness, Jesus is science, Jesus is being, Jesus is now. The statement 'Jesus is Lord' assumes that we all know the story of the Christian faith: the birth stories, John the Baptist, the miracles, the death, the resurrection, all held together in an understanding that is common to all people. For someone who subscribes to post-modernism to use the slogan 'Jesus is Lord' is like a survivor of the sinking of the Titanic queuing up in New York for the return journey home on the same ship.

The last performances of the third group in front of the cameras came home to roost this morning. I had never realised just how long the camera focuses on someone while their name and current employment are read out by the person chairing the session. The penny dropped when a curate with very large ears, who was trying to sit still enough to convince us all he wasn't terrified, appeared on camera. It was at this point that the entire veneer of the situation melted and comedy took over. He was very, very funny; he looked as though he'd been caught in the spotlight and had completely frozen. I'm afraid every word he said after that reduced me to a giggling wreck.

I was trying to keep a low profile at breakfast when this comic genius came and sat next to me; he didn't speak for a minute or so and then he asked how I thought it had all gone yesterday afternoon.

I have always admired Herbert Long. He had set out to be a serious actor, taking on some very weighty roles, and he was phoned up one day by Blake Edwards who offered to buy him lunch. Long was a little confused, but he accepted and they small-talked for an hour or so. Then Blake Edwards said to Long he had enjoyed his last film, in which Long played some eminently serious role, but that he had to tell him he found him very, very funny.

Snowdonia tomorrow.

It's pouring with rain. Everything is wet. The grey mountains are broken by brilliant white lines of fast falling water; the clouds have settled, hiding all the summits, compressing the space between the land and the sky. The Llanberis Pass snakes up eight miles in from the coast, the road perched between slate walls which tumble into ever-bigger blocks sleeping in sublime chaos, threatening the wall which hems in the road.

The Pen-y-Gryd is where we stay. When we arrived here wet and dripping six years ago there was a fire on the inside. It's the place where they all trained for the Everest expedition. Edmund Hillary signed the ceiling in the bar along with all the others; that must have been an evening and a half, that one. There are photos of these people everywhere, wearing huge boots and goggles that appear to have been designed to be complicated; they sit in grottoes crammed with ancient mountaineering kit which fill in the small print that myth has removed. This is a secret place.

Bethsaida is described as a sorry place in the guidebooks. We cut through the back streets and jammed the car up on the verge. It was about a two and a half mile yomp up to the back of Carned Dafed. The top was lost in the clouds; there was the sound of water everywhere, pouring off the slopes, bulging in the moss that sticks to your feet. The slope was cluttered with rocks and bones, sheep that had fallen; they were in pieces everywhere after the crows and laughing ravens had feasted on them. We turned left into the clouds, up on to a knife edge, and then it all smoothed out on to the top, the wind whining – it could kill you. Carned Llewellyn was lost; you need to sweat to get there. It is nothing more than a moonscape. When you can't see more than ten yards your senses go with the endless grey granite; when the clouds broke for a moment, when the sun hit every droplet hanging in the air, you could see the speed of the moving sky, then we were really lost. It was open for a moment, then it all closed in again, shut in the whitewash.

We followed the compass to Yr Ellen. It's only 3,120 feet, a little lower than the rest. The view suddenly reappeared after a long scrambling path and there it was, golden valleys on both sides, a clear grass slope between the two. The God of these mountains is a million miles away from the villages that proclaim him, proclaim her. You cannot translate this extraordinary emptiness, extraordinary richness into suburbia. Contemporary Christianity thrives on concrete and glass, the word needs words; we have engineered God into sentences, tied him, tied her up in theology. What do we say then to these mountains, to this mayhem, to this ice and sunshine? This is the point where the institution fails, simply because this place has no need of it, where all the cosy theories steeped in coffee, in house groups, worship committees, building development programmes and millions of miles of liturgy break down completely. Up there you lose your words in the wind.

The Church of England has become urban-derived. Our spirituality, our sense of self, if you were to put it on a map where would it be? What sort of town would best describe what it is? Carshalton, Durham, Tunbridge Wells, Peterlee? It's more middle-class than the middle of nowhere. No wonder the church could not respond to the environmental movement's pleas that the land, the air, the rain was sacred: that's not what we are actually about. We are lost in sex and cement.

We have all colluded in the delusion that says so little when factory farming is justified on economic grounds, when in the name of progress tarmac displaces ptarmigan. There is a real contradiction here, because while the village communities in this country have been stripped of their independence by the prevailing thinking that dictates factory shopping and urban cool, while local shops and banks have been closed over the last thirty years at a pretty steady rate, the Church of England has stuck resolutely by the villages of this country, at what has been a great personal cost to the priests and the structures that support them. It has stood against the fashionable thinking of urban dependence. Even though we have, in our usual fashion, been appallingly bad at explaining why we have chosen to do this, here we are. The differences between what is termed a successful urban church – and that is the model of excellence we in the countryside are usually offered – and what happens on a Sunday morning in Harlton, are poles apart. The Evangelical model, full of model Evangelicals who tend to live elsewhere and have very little emotional investment in the community that lives around the church, is completely different from the rural church, which is very much based on the villages we serve. By its very nature it serves the local people. This may all look very quaint from the outside – the country parson involved intimately with the village – but as a model of care, the urban churches cannot really touch it. It is rooted in the dust that time leaves behind, dealing with, not so much dipping into, people's lives. At best, it is servant of all within the village. The city-centre churches in London, in Cambridge, necessarily create their own communities; in that sense the two churches are doing very different things, practically and theologically. I'm not at all taken with the self-creating model of ministry where the model is effectively superimposed on those who adhere to it, where church is sacrificed for churchmanship, ecclesia for ecclesiastical. Perhaps survival demands indifference; when you are fighting for your existence, which is what we are doing, then like the starving man everything is focused inwards.

Despite the dogged and sometimes touching determination of the Church of England in the small places, whichever way you look at it the last fifty years have been awful for Western Christianity. Having lost our nerve and our edge we have been driven closer and closer to the precipice of irrelevance. Maybe there, maybe out there on that ledge we will come to our senses. We've been so obsessed trying to locate the historical garden of Eden that we have been unable to move with the environmentalists' insistence that we are living in it. This planet *is* Eden, surely. Maybe when we have been stripped naked by the media, paraded as fools, we will realise how foolish we have been. Certainly postmodernism has no need of our grand theories; that has to be a bonus. Our imposition of morality, offering rescue from the rocks of our own creation, is also beginning to look pretty threadbare. Those disgruntled with modernisation will suggest that to focus on style rather than substance means the church is neglecting its true calling. The issue *is* style, the substance of our style, the way we communicate what we believe in: the church is obsessed with style. What we believe in hasn't changed really, but the style of our belief has become all-consuming; we have been fighting our own battles far, far away from the front.

Here's a typical example that arrived in the diocesan mailing this morning.

To priests of the Catholic tradition in the Diocese of Ely.
As a former chairman of the Federation of Catholic

September

Priests in the Diocese of Ely I am most grateful to the present membership for their courtesy in letting me know that from 15th September they propose to transfer their allegiance to the Society of Catholic Priests since that body, unlike the Federation, is prepared to accept women priests as members. From conversations I have had I feel there might be enough support to RELAUNCH FCP IN ITS TRADITIONAL FORM IN THE DIOCESE and have been in touch with the secretary who has offered his encouragement.

It goes on to say in much the same undertone that if you are interested, get in touch. We are embroiled in it really, all of us: politics, camps, camps in camps.

In this mêlée the words of Christ are translated before he has actually spoken them. Can they still mean what tradition has said they mean? This generation will find no relevant contemporary meaning unless it is prepared to read them afresh, speak them afresh, claim them as their own, unravel them from history. Every hair on your head is numbered, not a sparrow falls to the ground without my Father in heaven knowing about it. The lilies of the fields are far more radiant than King Solomon. These are not quaint poetic ramblings, although their meaning has been reduced to poetry. Those were words spoken by a man who came closer to God than any of us could either cope with or dare. They are words of steel. To put them into harvest festivals mixes messages. Harvest festivals almost celebrate a Victorian harvest: they are earthed in small fields, they insist upon a halcyon dream that is lovely to believe in, pinafored and petticoated, smelling of sweet hay, flagons of cider made from apples piled high in carts pulled by kind horses. That may be what we want; it may make us warm inside. But unless we can deal with the piggeries and the pesticides, the suicides, the antibiotics, we are doing no more than advertising a product that does not exist. As a priest you inherit all this, you inherit models that are tried and tested certainly, but for the most part are completely out of date. We can be no more than guardians of a golden past as long we continue to celebrate it. I took a harvest assembly at a private school this morning; we managed to name ten birds, five butterflies and about eight trees. We then reached the fish. There was this small boy at the front who had said nothing, practically waving his arm – he must have been no more than five. 'What fish can you name?' I asked. He looked me straight in the eye. 'Smoked salmon,' he said.

October

We have no money. It's Tuesday evening. The pay cheque came in last week; it's all gone. After one hundred and forty quid is deducted for the car loan we are left with £1,033.36. We get the house – a celebration in breeze blocks that somehow manages to creak, complaining when you walk around upstairs – and a quite wonderful garden. Being out in the sticks means we need two cars. Insurance and road tax comes to around seven hundred and fifty quid a year, then there's servicing and all the rest of it. The list is endless: five hundred quid to fill the oil tank, all the other stuff as well. The main problem is one of extravagance. We live hand to mouth. Jacs and I never get to go out together. This is partly due to the fact that we have four young children who are experienced in shredding babysitters. Jane and Roderick come over once in a while; they are brilliant and always refuse to be paid, but that's usually when we are out on official business

The combination of no money and awful hours does without doubt take its toll. It does get bloody; vicars work incredibly antisocial hours. I have meetings most evenings. There's the old theory that you should structure your day into three sections and work two of them. This is totally unworkable; the workload is nothing other than enormous. More often than not I start at around 8 in the morning and finish at 10 at night. I could tread water and just do what is necessary, follow the print, but it doesn't lead anywhere really. There is no long line of things that have to get done. Yes, you have to preach a sermon on Sundays, bury the dead, marry lovers. I'm still amazed that people think this is a one-day-a-week thing. Maybe we give that impression, sitting in our studies; I'm sure that is where we have gone wrong. It's not about making your mark on a parish. It is actually, at best, enabling people to find God, to hear the still small voice of calm, that calms all of us, to take risks with reality, to believe that God is truly love. Priests are no more than caveats. You do have to sacrifice yourself; once you wrap a dog-collar round your neck you give up being you. You become unimportant; people don't see the person, they see the parson, they see the priest. To be honest, individual personality simply gets in the way most of the time and you are left with these two people, the person you are and the person you have become. The tension between the two is fantastic; the role is so seductive, but role-playing simply means I cannot handle it. My masculinity, my sexuality is surrendered; it becomes unimportant and is redefined in the whites of other people's eyes. We are not meant to desire, you see, we are not supposed to look down the line that leads into the dark along the skin formed when thighs are crossed, we are not meant to get angry. Are these extremes? These situations make priests vulnerable because more often than not we fail because we are male, because we are female, because none of us is strong enough really to carry that cross.

This plays havoc with your self-esteem and it's at this point the role comes in handy. But it is no more than a drug, a very addictive drug indeed, and there are lots of us addicted to it. We wave our arms from the pulpit, we smile when we need to. But thankfully it doesn't work at home. That oasis usually carries the shame of those things that I am not expected to be: sexual, masculine, aggressive, morose. When the role takes over completely and the gap between the person and the priest becomes a gulf, then you are in real trouble. Some people end up as Jekyll and Hyde. Marriage has to be a good thing, but reconciling the public person and the private person is not always easy. Was there this gap when the disciples stood around Jesus Christ as he cured people, when he spoke those beautiful lines on the mountain? Did they look up and sense at that point that they had nothing to do with him, or was it the same person? Maybe what the elders from the temple were attempting to do, when they asked him about Caesar's head on the coin – should they pay tax – was to separate the two: they couldn't. Maybe he was so incredibly charismatic because he was ultimately always offering people the truth about himself. Imagine an absence of self-interest, no agenda, no spin, no role play. In this society spin has become almost respectable; we know that politicians are playing games with us so we care for them less. The media have the dubious gift of whipping us all into a frenzy over the fact that the grass is growing; Christ seems to have had completely the opposite effect on people. But in those eyes, those words, was eternal truth and it must have been overwhelming. The trouble with eternal truth is that it is dangerous. Lies lose their shine very quickly; the angle you take to spin the best lie is usually your weakest point. If people think you are trying to hide something you are in fact offering them an invitation to find out what it is. There is nowhere to hide here. I completely underestimated the public nature of the priest's role – your failings become public property and you are carried completely by others. That in itself is always very humbling.

There was an American artist on television last night. I don't remember his name; he had a face swollen by pills. A plastic tube arched over each of his cheeks up into his nostrils. Every so often he would cough, his lungs contorting as the cystic fibrosis he suffered from marched him towards a death he said he didn't hate. Among other things his art was a celebration of decay. He had sculptured a face on half an apple and then videoed it as it withered and became the fascination of flies. Yes, it was extraordinary, very, very powerful. The artist who inspired us also entertained us with his own naked form, either tied to a bed or strung up hanging by the ankles for his own particular pleasure, which was maximum pain. Maybe Adam's hand reaching over to take the apple from Eve is not this dreadful fall that we have had to deal with, it is the ultimate demonstration that we choose sin and that it is our choice, my choice, your choice. To saddle us all with the concept of original sin seems increasingly alien to me from the perspective of a God of love. We are in the process of blaming God for our own decisions, for a numbness we feel when we cheat, when we lie, when we commit adultery, when we murder. It is a perversion to blame God for the things we have chosen to do and for our capacity to do them. At some point you have to stop blaming your parents for the way you behave. It's all too easy to never grow out of it, though, and spend our lives denying the freedom actually to do anything about it. We become defined by these flaws rather than our own extraordinary beauty.

Michael Meacher is considering a three-year ban on genetically modified crops. It seems we now need genetically modified crops because so many of them have become resistant to pesticides. I couldn't believe that's what the bloke from the consortium pressing the government to give them the licences to grow these things was saying. He's right; he was also saying that genetically modified crops would allow more weeds to grow and for slightly longer, producing more insects and in turn hopefully an increase in the population of birds that the agrochemical industry have managed to slaughter over the last thirty years. It's incredible really that genetic modification has now been cited as saving us all from the horrific mistakes the agrochemical industry has been making for years. The use of pesticides has been a catastrophic failure for all of us, has laid dead birds at our feet. It seems rather incongruous that we are being asked to trust the same people who sold us pesticides as progress. As human beings we modify, we manipulate iron from stone, clunch into cement; it is perhaps part of our creative nature. The problems arise when we assume that we are god. God, however, I believe, treats us as if we are sacred. Problems, huge problems, arise when we treat this world as if it isn't.

On this side of the hill in Haslingfield we are also guinea pigs for another experiment, this time one concocted by Rugby Cement, aided and abetted by the Environment Agency. Never before has a more misleading name been given to a government department.

SLF, sanitary landfill, is the wonder substance, a combination of the residue that's left from the chemicals that dry-clean your clothes and other delightful ingredients, burned under licence to create the heat needed to make cement. SLF was previously dumped and then some bright spark said, if this is highly inflammable we can sell it, and so they do. At the public meeting which was called to discuss Rugby's application to burn more of this stuff, the same old adversaries took to the stage, took to their familiar corners: the environmentalists versus the industrialists. We spent two hours debating whether SLF was actually safe to burn, which proved beyond doubt that nobody actually knows. Then Bob's your uncle, ten weeks later the

Environment Agency gives Rugby Cement a licence to burn more of it.

It's Sunday tomorrow. Anne, a student from one of the theological colleges in Cambridge, is preaching.

We started four minutes late in Haslingfield this morning. There are two churches in Haslingfield: the church at the front and the church at the back. The church at the front has been in severe decline since the church at the back took up residence. The church at the front is what everyone thinks the Church of England is: over fifty, power-driven by the purity of a vision where the world runs on time and the service is overseen by a patrician soul who gently but ruthlessly upholds etiquette, guards the structures and strictures of the Church of England, drinks sherry and keeps bees. They want a hierarchy where age and experience are rewarded with authority. Sounds horribly like the Church of England. Sermon references to Rik Mayall, farmers high on chemicals, the time when I smoked cannabis, kissing and Andy Warhol are not encouraged. Most of these people had a sixties bypass. With the onslaught of Jim Morrison, the Monkees, miniskirts and Harold Wilson, they fled into church. There they have stubbornly stayed. Make no mistake, they are a force to be reckoned with; for a start, as things currently stand, they run the Church of England: they are backbone. Outside the big cities, they are the fêtes, the remembrance service, the gift day, the treasurer. They make the tea, they arrange the flowers, they clean the church, they cut the grass, they make anonymous donations. They stand up for what they believe in completely, they stand together and they are not going to be mucked around by some two-bit Johnny-come-lately who paints his gates purple, smokes roll-ups and is more often than not late for everything. Individually they are amusing, kind and generous. En masse, they can become a recurring bad dream.

Their recurring bad dream, however, sits behind them: breast-feeding mothers, children that throw tantrums in the most solemn part of the services, parents who let their offspring wander up and down the aisle, young married couples who slouch in the pews, invariably with their arms round each other. The respect has gone; these people come in spite of the institution. They are not the grass-cutters of the future, but they are the church. It is actually God who has changed somehow. The Father of the front and the Father of the back are actually very, very different. The only place where all this is reconciled is when we take communion. There we are equal and it is the best part of the service. When we come together at the altar none of this makes sense and none of it matters. It is still extraordinary, it is still beautiful. I admire the front of the church first of all because they have put up with me; the ones that are left are asking difficult questions. They actually want the institution to be an entity which commands respect, they want bishops to be important, they want cropped choir boys, certainty and order, because that's what they have invested in and it all becomes self-defining. If the church is a joke then so are they. If we started to stand up for justice for the Third World, if we were to make a noise about the unbridled megalomania of genetic modification, the moral Stalinism of the tabloids, the disgrace of pollution, the bankruptcy of American cinema, the church would not only be in danger of undermining its own power base but we would also undermine theirs, which is why we have been so silent. We would have to roll up our sleeves and brawl with the rest of them. Clearly that is not our style. The declaration on homosexuality at the Lambeth conference was a great victory for the front of the church really. Here we are back in firm moral territory again, back on the rocks of certainty.

Before the spectacular fall of Christopher Brain, the self-styled leader of the nine o'clock service, I saw him interviewed on the television. In the days leading up to the nine o'clock service in Sheffield, he said, a group of about twenty of them would pile into the local church; they usually went and sat right at the front. He probably did realise what an incredibly threatening act that was. It was almost tantamount to invasion, which is what it turned out to be.

Anne preached very well. It's Peggy's funeral tomorrow.

Peggy had the most incredible hair. It was long and near enough blonde. She was eighty-one. Her house was just behind the vicarage here. She had no electricity and no running water. She'd been there since she was in her early teens. She was totally free of an admiration for material things. She saw and admired a beautiful world and was steeped in it. Free from the dreadful curse of materialism, she had nothing to prove. A Rolls Royce might have been grand, but she would never have been aware that she was actually sitting in one. She had no conception of what was cool and what wasn't; she didn't see it and so rendered it utterly inconsequential. Not through aggression: I never heard her bemoan the present or paint the past as a better place. She never once said, what is the world coming to? It is an awful line, that one; old people use it as a weapon, as a barb to tell you they're essentially unhappy with what they have become, that the present is pale when shone against the past. Peggy accepted you as you were, not as your job defined you, or the wealth we use to hide behind. She looked you straight in the eyes – not in a threatening way; she was actually showing you her heart. No, Peggy saw off the developers who would periodically roll up to try to price her house out of her; she never wanted anything else, she wasn't a hostage to fortune, to favour, to ambition, to finery. She took you, me and the world as it was. She left no ill-feeling, no guilt, no remorse behind her. She had the most beautiful garden.

She would have fallen below that awful poverty line; why do we have it? Poverty has raised some dreadful ghosts. We see them paraded before us, this roll-call of second-class citizens: travellers' children without shoes, caravans cradled underneath looming gas works, pensioners with the obligatory blanket, sitting in front of a bar heater, their faces as grey as their hair. If money is your God then poverty is hell. This creed is rattled out by the godless West, the self-styled saviours of the third world. Aid it's called, and it has done little more than bankrupt the recipients.

Jesus Christ refused to accept the age-old totalitarian edict that declares that those without money are poor, and he refused to go along with the other popular misconception that those with money are rich. It must have terrified the given order of the day. The fact that we continue to allow wealth to define status just goes to show how spiritually bereft we have become. Christ said none of it was necessary – our diamonds, our gold, our ridiculous palaces, ludicrous limousines – worthless all of them. Give them up, he said. Be strong enough not to need them, and whatever you do don't let them make you unhappy, and even worse don't let them make you feel that you have failed, don't be defined by them; they will lie to you every time. It's cool to be poor, that's what he said.

It's beautiful now, long autumn shadows. The grass in front of the shed is a furious green. At its edge is a huge holm oak. The bough has split into three main sections. The crown spills out this immense dome, everything is hidden in it. Occasionally you catch the blue lapels of a jay, flashes of squabbling magpies and shining rooks. The squirrels strangely chose the eaves of the house to rear their young, instead of the tree; there is a drey up on the top stitched into a spray of twigs, just under the point where the leaves begin in earnest. The male squirrel is almost brown, the white fur on his stomach seems to have taken on a nicotine yellow. He casually sat there eating an acorn yesterday as the nature club from the school all peered up at him from the undergrowth. We went round the garden together looking at the buddleia where the butterflies bloom and the cabbages which their caterpillars have enjoyed more than we have.

It was fifteen hours yesterday; I started at 8 and finished just before 11. I always try to go to bed without tomorrow insisting on being heard; it is an impossible job to do properly. Priests work when everyone else plays, and when they're playing there's always the suspicion that they should be working. We're meant to have one day off a week but I can't refuse funerals, and if a Friday is the only day the family can manage I always take them. The PR from having to find someone else from another parish to take a funeral would be awful; they are working just as hard as I am, so adding to that is madness. But it is not just the standing at the front at the funeral. Everyone reacts to death in different ways. Some people really go to pieces, they just unravel in front of you. This is actually a very good thing because it means they're able to express the grief they are feeling. Other people contain it; there is always guilt in those tears, you see. The tears demand so much from us, and then four months down the line they start to crack. There are others: they are usually the ones who can reconcile themselves to the fact that it was actually beautiful, who simply accept it immediately. But we all react in our own way. There is no script; you just have to deal with individual grief individually. Death always asks such huge questions. I had never been to a funeral before I actually took one. I was terrified; people that don't go to church remember mistakes that priests make. I have made one dreadful mistake so far. One afternoon I went round to a house where a man in his seventies had died. I had taken a funeral in the morning. At the end of the conversation in the front room I suggested we say a short prayer. I got the name wrong; I prayed for the man that had been buried in the morning. They were really upset, it was nothing other than terrible; they were incredibly gracious about it all, but at that point, that critical point, I let them down. They were worth a great deal more than that, and I shouldn't have done it.

London tomorrow, the Churches Advertising Network; we'll see how Easter is shaping up.

Easter was dull, pale, neutral; you would have walked past it. There was nothing about it that would have opened your heart. The only question you might have asked, if it had appeared at the bottom of your fish and chips, was, is God really like this, safe, dull, pale, neutral? So we're going to start again. We are trying to please two audiences at the moment, and we usually end up worrying both of them. The posters can't be too bright, too bold, too bolshie, otherwise the front of the church won't buy them, and if the front of the church won't buy them we don't have any money to put up the socking great billboards. Maybe we should produce kind and sweet posters for the church notice boards so that they're bought in droves and then with the money we have made produce some thorny work for the high street. At the moment we simply end up every time advertising the church. We looked at the possibility of using doubt, the doubting atheist, to prey on those doubts, manipulate them, shine them, to turn the tables so that doubt wasn't the shadow of this divine madness we call faith, nor the legacy of an emptiness fermented in lager, chanted on Saturday afternoons and recited in the mantra of the free market. The church tends not to go in for vulgar advertising. The Churches Advertising Network is a rump; the traditional strategy has been to allow, to encourage Christians to spread Christianity, God speaking in our eyes, in the way we love and in what we love. So, as you've probably noticed, the communications revolution has passed us by.

The English always squirm at what they see as the commercialisation of their faith as offered by the Anglican Americans: chapels of love, priests that look like Elvis and all of that, drive-in marriages, posters that say 'Speak in tongues in three hours'. The Church of England is usually entertaining for different reasons. There is a wonderful innocence that is suspicious of advertising, that quite rightly says it's manipulative. Of course it is – it's meant to be. All persuasion that is aimed to persuade you that you are a child of God is also essentially manipulative. There is one beautiful exception however: the communication that hopes to persuade you of nothing, the action of love that has nothing other than your own interests at heart. If Christianity was pervaded through, by that love, totally free from persuasion of any kind, totally free of a vested interest of any kind, then we would see some fireworks. The institution is failing to deliver this: Christianity has become something you think rather than something you do. It has, through the essentially intellectual structure of the church, become a religion of the mind, not of the soul.

During the heyday of the Roman empire it was Christians that were offered to the wild animals in the amphitheatres, it was Christians who were pitted against trained gladiator killers to provide the entertainment. No wonder the Christian faith eventually won over the Roman empire. You were guaranteed crucifixions in every amphitheatre every Saturday afternoon.

That ultimately must have been very persuasive indeed. What is it that distinguishes those who go to church from those who don't today? We have become pale, we have become dull. Those who are waiting for our demise, though, are in for a nasty shock. When we have sold our bishops' rings for a bottle of communion wine, when we have closed the doors of our churches because they have become unviable, when priests such as myself are back in the gutter where we belong, when we have sold our silver chalices, when we have given up all claim on power and social sweetness, when we have nothing left other than God – which is the truth of it – then perhaps we will need nothing other than God.

It's been a day for dying. Everything seemed to melt, become empty, the colours declined. It's better now it's dark. I've moved into the shed; there's a radiator that creaks and the whole thing pitches in high winds. The vicar's study is an institution in itself, but the study in the house is jammed with Batman, coloured bricks and books. I didn't move out so our children could have a den of their own – I moved out to protect them and my wife. There is one great tradition that you should never lose and that is that the vicar's door is always open. Out on the fabulous Fens we had a lot of callers, people sometimes dossed in the garage. But there were times when this was dangerous, times when people were so drunk, so stoned and so angry that an explosion would have really put everyone at risk, most of all them.

Also your family are drawn into the dramas, the tears, the pain; what separated Prince Charming singing, 'So this is love' on Walt Disney's *Cinderella* from a man threatening loudly to hang himself on the nearest tree was just a plywood wall. I used to get tense because if the shit really hit the fan, and that's just a matter of time, then we would all be very vulnerable. Priests do still die because safety nets rip or people quite naturally go out of their way to avoid the mesh. We have no truncheons, no CS gas, no combat training, and I would never accept it ever, but I cannot knowingly put our children at risk, so I'm in the shed. It's been a revelation; we still get travellers but not nearly as many. The last man had the most beautiful face; there was not one piece of his skin that wasn't lined. He had been in the merchant navy for over forty years, he said, now he was on the road. He was on his way to the Fens to pick fruit. He thought very carefully before he spoke, his words were quiet, he said he never drank alcohol and that too many men had been ruined by it. He had lunch and I drove him to Ely. It was as far as he wanted to go.

There is nothing romantic about sleeping under a bridge or trying to persuade the social services to give you a fiver. But in some people who, for whatever reason, choose to live with nothing or have to live with nothing, there is a grace that few of us can touch. I met this man called Rod out on the Fens; he lived with the rats running over the carpet in a mayhem of fights and hash. Once in a while he would take off to Ireland and work as a gardener. He would leave with nothing and come back with nothing. Occasionally he would sneak in for the last ten minutes of a Sunday service, but that God was light years away from the Jesus Christ he sometimes quietly spoke about, the man that he said walked with him on the road.

We have totally lost a contemporary description of Christ, we simply do not have one. We simply do not have one that makes any sense or speaks to this world. We tend to go in for the historical models; these models are still very powerful but they really are no match for the present. Perhaps that is why biblically based Evangelical Christianity appears to be on the rise; it offers certainty, yes, but for a low return. The

Alpha course set up by Holy Trinity Brompton is about *my* soul, *my* response, nobody else's. What has changed, other than the numbers? I am given permission to think about my relationship with God and at the end of the day that is all that seems to matter. It is spiritual materialism. It leaves in its wake carpets, chairs, toilets and overhead projectors. You'll end up on an island; it is about self-preservation, not self-sacrifice.

They are building palaces fit for a king. Sadly, that is what churches have become. I'm not sure our king wants to be a king at all, least of all to be treated like one. That is how we continually, foolishly, describe Christ. The word has lost its power and potency, thankfully; it has become a historical toy, a tourist trinket, the blue blood defrocked and defaced by millions of miles of ink. The future head of the Church of England is cast as the court jester by too many people who are clearly keen to take his place. The position of the monarch as head of the Church of England may have been politically necessary, and may give the front of the church some certainty, but it will not only compromise the church but also compromise him. It's time we both shook hands and went our separate ways.

Amazing piece in *The Times* a while ago – this is Catherine Lucas's description of God: 'It was like dropping through a trapdoor into darkness and I found myself in what I can only describe as a sea of sparkling energy. I was conscious, but nothing, including my body, had any form or structure. At first I was astonished and then I realised that whereas before I had experienced the presence of God in all things, this was God, at least this is what people call God for the sake of calling it something. Finally I understood God is not an old man in the sky, it is a limitless ocean of consciousness, of unmanifest energy and the source of everything in existence from the largest planet to the smallest insect.' Beautiful words. Have you ever glimpsed that, sensed that? I'm sure it is what we all sense. The trouble is we want to bottle it and own it, and we wind ourselves through the same rituals in the mere hope of touching it again. It is so precious, so extraordinary, so overwhelmingly true that people fight tooth and nail to have their own reference points for this experience maintained, which is why the church and change have always been at odds; it's always been a tortured business. But we simply can't turn God on like a tap, though that's what we try to do. We meet to conjure up this limitless ocean of consciousness. We need to plug into it in the hope that we might glimpse it. It's there all the time, it hasn't gone away. We don't really help people to find it, not really, do we? We give them our old map and say, this is the only way. We have behaved as if we own the patent and not as if we are part of it. We have proclaimed Christ king and ourselves as courtiers, made his mother a queen. Thankfully now this makes us ridiculous rather than important, as I'm sure it used to. We gave him jewels and a golden crown largely so we could see our own reflection in it.

November

We're meant to be in France. My father-in-law died last year; he had always wanted us, the whole family, to go away somewhere together, so we're doing it now and he's paying for it. One of our children is not well so we've postponed everything for a couple of days. It's hard to imagine a hot place; autumn has really set in, the leaves on the road to Barton are a thousand yellows. Each morning you can see more of the wood as they lose their grip, as the first frosts leave them far too brittle for the reaping wind. It all depends how you see it: biology in action, the drama of the fierce and beautiful struggle for life, a beautiful war where for the moment we are the victors, where we have won the right to cut off sharks' fins and throw the body overboard, to eat skylarks and Kentucky fried chicken, to gaze at snakes in cages and destroy the fragile and subjugate the weak in the name of food and humanity. Do we want to be the victors over unruly nature? What sort of regime are the so-called 'defeated' offered? You are yourself the god of science, you are the god of genetic engineering, you are the god of every sparkling Lamborghini. How many times have you been told that all this is done in your name, that 'we take the same amount of care of the big things as well as the little things'?

Great advertising makes you the hero, not the product; you know the script, you've read it often enough.

John Main said, 'Know from your heart from your own experience that you were created for an infinite expansion of the spirit': one of the most dangerous contemporary sentences written. Maybe Christ saw the world continually in those moments, while we are only able to glimpse grandeur when our breath is taken away, when we forget who and where we are, when everything is caught in a timeless frame. Prayer is a ludicrous thing really, totally unscientific, an insult to logic. The places we go, the voices we hear, the colours we see are impossible to picture; they can only be translated through our breakable words. Surely we do not need to prove that God exists, the logical will never get a logical explanation. Surely God is as much a part of the theories we call proof as the process, the seconds in our being that we spend journeying towards whatever conclusion we might have reached; the conclusion itself.

Travel is a great privilege. There is undoubtedly a thin line between tourism and voyeurism. The south of France was dry, the mushrooms in the woods did not rot, they simply became moistureless statues. The patterns set solid in the gills of the wonderful parasols that seemed to grow everywhere. Did the French learn to ride bicycles in a certain style? It's very different from the English, head down, hurrying against the headwind. The French tend to aim their knees outwards and ride at an unconcerned pace. They give the impression that a bumble bee might upset their balance. The town was a poodle paradise, little dogs everywhere on long leads. Why is it that fat owners tend to have fat dogs? There are also some very impressive moustaches, great big handfuls of hair slapped between the nose and mouth. The Stalin style seemed to be in vogue. The policemen are fantastic – most of them are a cross between Alvin Stardust and a South American dictator – tight trousers, mirrored sunglasses, loads of silver chains coming out of impossible pockets. The guy at the airport was great. He sidled over, spread his legs as if he was about to mount a horse, then stood there for at least fifteen seconds, staring at the blue disabled parking logo where, out of desperation, we had ended up. He then looked at me. I think I explained in appalling French that we would only be there for two minutes to load up our luggage. His response was total silence. He then very slowly brought his hand up to his chin and simply sidled off. The whole process took about three minutes. You can't really go away with four young children and have what is commonly termed a holiday – it's more of an endurance test. Children thankfully do what children do: make camps, shoot people with sticks, fight, vomit, wake you up at five in the morning on the pretence they have a wasp in their ear, complain on the beach that the sand is scratching their toes. This could have taken place in a house where they had their bearings and weren't running into the walls and using the bidet as a rubbish bin and more.

Luton at eight o'clock wasn't glamorous. We hacked through the generous rain and made it home by 10. I packed a bag, got up at 6, drove down to Heathrow and flew over the exact spot where we were staying twelve hours earlier, and arrived in Rome on the DCOs conference. DCO stands for Diocesan Communications Officer. Every diocese in theory has one and some of them have an extremely torrid taste in jumpers. It's a packed four days, ending with a reception at the Vatican ambassador's residence which, I'm holding out high hopes, will closely resemble that spectacularly dreadful ad for those even worse chocolates. The irony is we've all been told to dress sensibly for that, no jeans and T-shirts. What happens if some people take this as a green light for their favourite jumper? We'll have to wait and see. We have not been encouraged to leave the abbey where we are staying, essentially a centre built around a fountain where St Paul is supposed to have met a very grisly end. Apparently the main road is wall-to-wall with ladies of the night. We've also been warned at least eight times about the supremely gifted pickpockets who can spot a loaded wallet from fifty yards. Not that many Anglican priests have such things as loaded wallets.

The director of the Anglican centre in Rome who came and talked to us after the pasta said some very fine things. He spoke passionately about the heritage of Anglican Christianity and how a large part of that heritage is actually from the Catholic tradition. Although the Church of England went with empire and, in many cases, before it, its traditions and ways are really only a very small part of global Christianity. He also said that we have now reached a point where only two per cent of practising Anglicans actually come from England; the rest are spread all over the world. The church in England may be dying as things currently stand but Anglicanism is clearly very much alive. The point was also made that we have lost our spirituality. I agree. It has been crippled by committees who for the most part have shamefully little to show for endless hours that they have spent discussing this and that. If they were performing we would not be in the position we are in now.

There has to be a difference between the sacred and secular. We have laid our cloaks down at the feet of the secular in an attempt to ingratiate ourselves with fashionable thinking. We have been wringing our hands together to try to make people like us, understand us. It's madness. The Catholics in the Vatican – Bruce Ruddock told us – think in centuries. We have all been sucked into seconds. No wonder then that contraception is still outlawed within the Catholic faith; it's going to be ludicrous when viewed from the perspective of a condom dispenser. It's so easy, isn't it? Put your money in, press the button, you don't have to think. Far from inspiring caution in people, the AIDS virus hasn't stopped us having sex; we can all now rest assured that we can have safe sex. Marvellous – you don't have to change your behaviour, you can screw as many people as you like as long as you're wearing a condom. Nothing has to change.

This is a wild and roaring city. I have never seen such sunglasses, the Romans wear them so well. The contrasts between the English college, the Catholic seminary where we had lunch today, where the rooms were full of fine and delicate faces, and the heaving hustle of the streets were shocking. We started the day at St Peter's. It is a massive empty room, the walls are gaudy, holding outsize saints – their plaster and marble eyes tell you no secrets. There are confessionals with little white signs above them telling you the language that's available. We were there for Mass at 9. I took communion, took the bread from the Catholic priest. Standing next to him was a very bored altar boy. I know I'm not meant to take Catholic communion, I've never taken it before, but I've been wanting to have it for some time. The idea that we can't, that it is forbidden to share the body and blood of Christ, that for me to take this from Catholic hands is wrong, I cannot accept. How can we claim to support one another, to be sympathetic, empathetic, call it what you will, if you are separated at the altar? It is religious apartheid, religious racism, there is too much blood on that carpet. I lost it completely afterwards; somehow in that impersonal room there is a great sense of God, the presence of God.

We carry so much pain with us all the time, we all do. Part of Jesus on the cross recognises that pain in all of us, the pain we endure, the pain we have to endure as human beings. We think we are being so strong by dealing with it, by carrying on, but for most of us we carry it round on a ball and chain. We are so weak that we cannot cry when we should and it becomes gratifying, self-defining, to take another punch in the face and carry on walking, carry on talking. People cry in churches because they are letting that pain go, they are letting it out. They are giving it to God who really is the only being strong enough to take it, to take it all.

After Mass we were taken to the Gregorian University: three and a half thousand students from 140 countries, studying everything from theology to communications. The Catholics take communications very seriously; they have radio stations all over the world. Communication is a subject, a discipline, along with ethics, the sum of sociology and the rest of it. After lunch I hit the vegetable market; there's no other way of saying it. Some of the women, some of the men are extraordinarily beautiful. These raging blue eyes, the colour of the sea that catch you for a second and then fly off again are everywhere. I don't understand this language, I couldn't ever roll up on the Lambretta and stop the engine in a manner that attracted everyone's attention. Everyone heard him before they saw him, it was a grand entrance. He was about six foot two with terracotta skin, Police sunglasses and the confidence, as Tom Sawyer would say, of a man holding four aces. His teeth were perfect.

The English don't preen – it's not the done thing. We're not allowed to take pleasure in removing our nasal hair and cutting our toenails, we're not encouraged to pout our lips. What is a practical matter for the English, the Italians have turned into an art form, and it shows. We borrow their suits, don't we, drool over their Ferraris, put our feet in their shoes?

Back at the abbey things became horribly normal again. We spent one and a half hours talking about process, which is short for power, authority and responsibility. The communication officers of the Church of England have very little. The centre does not seem to know what the dioceses are doing, and the dioceses do not know what the centre is planning. It was a disgrace really. I was hoping we would discuss how to take on the media. The *Sunday Times* ran a totally misleading torrid little piece about the Archbishop of York supposedly having a go at the Archbishop of Canterbury. It was designed and written to disturb and destroy. Because we're in such a shambles, they get away with it all the time; it was so far from the truth that it was a joke, but another joke at our expense, another chip of credibility lost in the mire. We ought to be talking about how we can communicate the love and grace of God, how we can end the media's obsession with our sexuality. But we talked about process, the outcome of which is another day in London to talk some more about process: who owns what, who's accountable to whom. This really should have been sorted out fifty years ago. I rashly suggested that we hire a professional to conduct a communications audit. The response from the chair was that he or she would probably need psychotherapy afterwards. Everybody laughed. It's not actually that funny though, is it?

I went back to the café yesterday, where the bloke rolled up on the Lambretta. The faces in the market were still there. A woman played the violin as we ate; it should have been a cliché but her toes were filthy. Did she ever think it would come to this, wandering in the market playing for the cafés with a rusty bow; had she ever dared see herself in diamonds and silk watching the last of a blue sun on an exclusive Moroccan terrace? She let you believe that through the chaos of colours, lettuces, ceps and flowers, the trembling bells, you had arrived somewhere; the music had formed another layer, filling up your soul.

We had the papal audience this morning, this wizened figure in white standing up on the back of a Land Rover was paraded round the crowd and deposited on what looks like a dentist's chair, which sat empty under what resembled half a French country railway station canopy. The crowd, which must have numbered about nine thousand, had come from all over the world; there were several choirs which occasionally burst into song. The most surreal moment was when a Bavarian quartet dressed in full lederhosen, had their turn and this lager music was piped through the PA system. We were all greeted in our own language and when your group was mentioned you waved wildly. Some of the groups had really gone to town on this waving moment and had either bought flags or what resembled 'Jukebox Jury' score cards. One Spanish group appeared to have been given green and white feather dusters which they all raised at the same time. He did look frail, but he has a kind face; he looks like your favourite grandfather. It was basically an international rollcall; after that we had a blessing and that was it. It was a glorious shambles, the Swiss Guards standing around in their torn trousers and the Italian police looking as hip as possible.

The Sistine Chapel was frightening. To get to it you have to walk through corridors lined with statues all missing arms and heads, then there are rooms full of paintings. God in the sky, saints held in a vain mirror mimicking Adam – they must have spent a great deal of time pumping iron to prepare themselves for martyrdom. This must have been Disneyland;

Michelangelo was a great entertainer. We all stood there looking up at the ceiling, bumping into each other, treading on other people's feet. He uses E-numbers as colours, angel delight as paint. We were voyeurs, tourists in a Renaissance heaven. This was a Renaissance theme park, Renaissance paint; we were looking up into a kaleidoscope. We all express our loneliness in different ways, this innate loneliness in all of us is the separation from God, from our home, our real home; we are clearly just visitors here. The wonderful flaw in the Sistine Chapel was Michelangelo's own dead skin, it was obvious ugliness and was empty of himself. He was showing us God's skin, and his own limitations in what he had painted. Clever man.

The ambassador's reception was everything it should have been. So was the ambassador. He had one of those faces that was made from off-cuts of wellington boots. He was tall, aquiline, born to rule. The house was set in the old city, the lawns were watered, the trees had high canopies. It was a place to fall in love. The only things missing were the Ferrero Rocher chocolates and a bloke with a sword taking the tops off champagne corks. We were all told to look respectable. We didn't manage it – the room was full of cheap suits and dog-food ties. None of us had the ambassador's effortless poise; essentially we all looked like we'd just got off a coach, which we had done.

The only time I have ever been entertained at her Majesty's pleasure it cost me more money than I had at the time. There were several dingy mornings reading some tragic graffiti in the emptiest and saddest rooms I have ever been in. There was no escape. Imagine if you were to dispense justice in grand rooms with beautiful views, on carpets, not concrete. One way or another we all paid for the whisky that was poured over the ice and splashed with Schweppes soda floating an electric lime.

We had no business there, not really. The Church of England is entirely compromised by the political establishment; we have become poodles. As the media has sussed completely, we make lousy guard dogs. No one is really sure any more what it is we are actually standing over.

I'm sure we are a convenient hole for the lost and lonely to jump into: I jumped. We are there to hold the line really, to underpin the excesses of mindless materialism with the perfume of heaven and love. The worst mistake we have made is to become fascinating for who we are rather than what we say or what we do. The Vatican is a business – it's a good business. The pope is the high priest. In a sense the Church of England's singular inability to market itself, its ludicrous and appalling public image, may well rescue it in the end from our culture where that is the only thing that matters. But the most dangerous aspect to all of this is the fact that there is no opposition. The media has presented us all with an ultimatum which reads sign up or sign out. The irony is we don't need any of it: the business community need it, politicians need it, the fashion industry needs it. The media mantra goes on, the great sixties prophecy has come true: turn on, tune in, drop out.

France was very quiet, nobody burning Guy Fawkes. England was sparkling at 7,000 metres, every single flash from every single firework. The paparazzi were going mad in Romford. It hasn't been a good week; the altar frontal from Little Eversden was stolen. I mentioned to the reporter that it would probably end up on a wall in America. It was beautiful. Very simple, hand-stitched wild flowers, that was all it was. The American priest who called me said my comment was disgusting and disgraceful and that he was going to report me to the bishop. I'm sure he will.

November

The day after that was the visiting conversation. My name is mud because I don't visit socially. I do visit socially – I visit quite a bit. I just don't visit the people who get sniffy about the fact that I don't visit. These are, frankly, people that go to church, who want the vicar to be the vicar of forty years ago, the man with one parish who could spend time with each individual church member, secure their confidence and, in doing so, their support. I would love a life like that, I'm just not able to express it in that way any more. I can understand that they feel short-changed: the institution that they loved is not behaving properly, it is not delivering the required standard. This must be particularly galling because they are, in the main, paying for it. But this vision of rural England does not exist any more and simply wanting it will not bring it back. I always leave a trail of disappointed people because I am unable to provide it. Saturday is generally an eight-hour day and Sunday I try to take the services and do no more in the afternoon unless people pop by. I know it's not a recipe for a good marriage and you have all the guilt that goes with that. I have since heard that it was inconsiderate of me to go away to Rome. Inconsiderate for whom? The only way you have to get away is actually to go away. You are isolated, there is no real support, you're on your own and to that extent you are very vulnerable, very vulnerable indeed. I don't get hacked off when I hear what's been said about me behind my back. I do get upset though when people are judged on their failings. The seedbed of complaints comes from within the churches themselves.

Criticism is fine – it's the lot of the parish priest with more than one parish. No one is really satisfied with that system. But it is the priests that ultimately carry the can for it. They have to absorb that dissatisfaction, the frustration that we cannot care as much as we would like to. You end up prioritising and carrying shadows. You find yourself making excuses because you know that you should be doing something but you also know you haven't got the time. If there is one thing I feel called to do, it is to build up the churches so they're places of mutual love and respect, where the needs of others are always placed before your own, where the love of God is tangible and the feeling of endlessness and the infinite that we are part of is felt by all; places where people are healed from what can be a brutal and bruising world, where we are all enabled by God, not disabled by an institution that imposes its culture and views as part of the price of belonging. But I am at a loss really, it's not working. I know I don't have the experience to call on – this is blind flight – but there is a great sense all around, with many other priests as well, that this actually isn't working, there is no real confidence in what ministry has become. We seem to be perpetually defending it, defending ourselves, our actions. We seem locked into a grid that is powered by candles, when the rest of the world runs on electricity.

Today we had mist – too thick for the wind. Everything slept, the trees glued still, the frost-frozen grass breaking when you trod on it. This morning a green woodpecker sat between the vegetable beds, pushing its beak down into the wet soil; it must have been about four shades of green with a red plume on its head. The last time I saw one that close was in the garden as a child. They fly at great speed. I wonder why they need to go so fast. There's a robin that has taken to waiting for us in the morning; we feed it bread. It was around in the summer, a fledgling then, with a song thrush's breast.

The Brownies showed up this evening. I think there were about twenty-six of them. I made a fire and we ate baked potatoes and drank hot soup. I wonder if they will remember it, how strong an experience it actually is. The sky was clear, covered with stars, could they hear them? The fire was angry, loud. I've really spent too much time in London – three of us have been going quite a bit. We're trying to find some interesting advertising for next Easter. The millennium campaign has been a disaster: hardly anyone has bought the posters or car stickers and without the churches buying them we can't afford to put posters up. So there will be none this Christmas. The campaign simply hasn't worked. The theme toted by the rivetingly titled Churches Millennium Group is 'New start', 'A new start with God', 'A new start for the world'. This might have had a gram or two of credibility if New Labour hadn't wooed us all with their polished promises. The exposure of the term New Labour has actually been enormous. What's interesting is that it's now fourteen months on, and it has just about sunk without trace. But the game has been played, to try to borrow the rules leaves us stirring pretty thin soup. There is also no budget to promote it. The strategy seems to be to shanghai the logo and the line on to as many church bandwagons as possible, the theory being that all these are setting off in different directions for the year 2000, so most of the country will see it. I have one question: what does it mean? It worked for the Labour Party, perhaps because we were promised fresh minds, fresh faces. The institution has been facelifted, there are suits and red roses. If you are indifferent about God, indifferent about Christ, the words 'New Start with God', I would imagine, have about as much potency as a cucumber sandwich. It's dull, it's predictable. But who is it aimed at? The line could well come to life if the Church of England were actually to take it on board. Rather than frying it in front of people, if we could demonstrate that we were taking it seriously, a reexamination of conscience, to refresh and revitalise the tired and moribund structures, to engage our society from a position of vulnerability rather than power. If we cannot demonstrate that we are taking the line as seriously as we would like everybody else to do then it will be business as usual on January the first, 2000; by July it will be as if nothing happened at all.

The Easter ad lacked some of the less obvious subtleties of the Christmas poster. We have a picture of Christ cast in the same pose as Che Guevara; underneath, the line reads 'Public enemy number one: discover the real Jesus of Easter'. It's good, it's very very good indeed. The media will go mad, the Bishop of Wakefield, the bishops' media guru, who can always be relied upon to say how outraged he is, will doubtless dive in on cue. But as a piece of communication which is trying to say this man was a revolutionary – a spiritual revolutionary – it is simple and memorable. Is there still an innate understanding of the sheer beauty and undiluted grace that God embodies? I don't know. Maybe we've given it up. The possibility may be we're simply giving up trying to be perfect. Maybe we've accepted failure as the more realistic platform to work from spiritually. If we accept that we can never possibly be like Christ, then we all have permission not to be like him; he can become a dream and waltz around in a white nightgown smiling at us. If we accept failure, accept that spiritually this man is beyond us, then accepting our cheap sins becomes easier and easier and we can hand justice over to judges, healing to doctors, love to Hollywood, food to neon food counters and they can deal us what we want. The dream of a just, free world where we are able to have our children playing in the streets, young women walking home alone at night, and old people without a battalion of locks on their doors, where the colour of our skin, our accents, our passports don't matter, seems to have gone. Two thousand years on and our streets are still places of fear and uncertainty. We buy locks and cars with a thousand codes. We've given in, it's become part of life. It's not freedom, it's slavery.

Anne was right when she preached – she spoke wonderfully. She said that we cannot solve the mystery of God, that our lives are part of the mystery, we are embroiled in it. To that end we are the substance of the mystery of the moment, all of us; the current flows through all of us. We all have the potential to love way beyond our means, to sense the great depth and purpose that we are in fact part of. No, we can't own it because it comes down to owning your face, your hands, owning the birds and the rain. The Israelites were given land; the mistake they made was believing it was theirs. What a relief, really, that none of it belongs to us. No, we can't have all the answers, and it's not going to be nice and rational, and thank God it makes no sense. The still small voice, the still small voice.

December

The Queen's Head in Newton is definitely one of the world's finest pubs. The back bar has a torn dart board and nicotine-coloured walls, the furniture is too big for the room, the tiles on the floor should be in a Victorian dairy. The windows in the main bar reach beyond to a small green island with one tree stuck in the middle of it. In the summer, people lie here, the cars slow down. In the winter the fire burns; if the wind blows hard some of it comes back down the chimney. The beer comes straight out of the barrel; it is the colour of the benches. This is sweet England. The road to it is up over a hill. In the spring the white smoke blossom billows on the hawthorn. Here you paint your inner years, laugh at your cuts and bruises. This is my retreat, a pint or two of glorious Adnams, a fresh fingerful of Old Holburn. There are no advertisements in churches for anyone other than Christ. Sometimes the odd Christian Aid poster breaks in. Imagine having a commercial break in the middle of the service, or a bit of carefully crafted product placement, a bottle of engine oil left on the altar.

On the way out of another meeting there was a man in a white robe standing next to the traffic lights in Parliament Square, holding a homemade banner, A4 pieces of paper glued together on a piece of wood: 'Unto us a child is born, unto us a saviour is given.' He aimed it at the cars waiting for the lights. His face didn't move at all. It was the complete antithesis of what we had been discussing for an hour – it was anti black-and-white photography, typefaces and winding body copy reeling you in. Maybe that's what made it so striking. We've all been corrupted by perfect images, beautiful men, beautiful women; you can talk to them, you can't touch them. They speak for money. For £500 an hour they will sell you anything, they will be anybody. It's an old trick: employ someone beautiful to do something ugly. There was Naomi Campbell lying on some floor with her legs almost open looking at me – what was she selling?

Father Christmas is an even stranger icon. The Victorian one used to wear green, then Coca Cola came along and gave him a red coat to match the colour of their logo, and it's been red ever since. He doesn't say much, does he? I think they've taken his brain away; this would account for the fact that he doesn't seem to do a great deal either, other than wander around department stores touching toasters and ladies' electric shavers, smiling gormlessly and saying ho, ho, ho: the soundbite Santa. St Nicholas has sold out, he's become disillusioned with love and peace and has taken a very lucrative job with the Chamber of Commerce. He still preys, on young children mainly, and the rest of us who have become too lazy and too busy to care either way. I used to have a girlfriend who lived on a sheep farm in Devon. The sheep instinctively understood what was going to happen when they arrived on a lorry at the slaughterhouse; the air must have smelt of blood. They all refused to leave the lorry. The slaughterhouse had the ultimate weapon – another sheep whose job was to walk up the gangplank, turn around and walk down again. Like sheep, they all followed. He was called Judas.

Christmas is upon us. We're having a Christingle service in Harlton tomorrow, there's another one in Haslingfield next Sunday. The Christingle service has become a permanent fixture in most churches. I'm always amazed at its popularity, why grown men should choose to stand around holding an orange with a candle in it singing 'Away in a Manger' is pretty much beyond me. The Christingle as a piece of symbolism doesn't really cut the mustard either, because muggins here has to explain what it all means at the same time every year. I've now just about got to grips with the fact that the orange represents the world, the red ribbon round it is the blood of Christ, the jelly tots and raisins jammed onto four exceedingly dangerous cocktail sticks are the fruits of the Spirit, and the candle is the light of Christ. But what it all means I'm afraid is a total mystery. I'm sure there is some sensible historical reason for all of it and I'm quite sure that makes no contemporary sense whatsoever. Perhaps when the lights go out and we are there in a circle with all the candles going, when in fact it's hard to see each other's faces, maybe that's intensely private and then in the half-light we can see just enough of God, just enough to let us know we're still loved, still cherished and that we're still there hanging on by this small red ribbon.

Christmas is an assault course – you have to hang on to God by your fingernails. You end up caught in an endless loop of 'Once in Royal David's City'; you become part of the Christmas card or just another turkey. You are walled in by the tradition and if you take a sledgehammer to it the falling masonry is liable to cripple you.

The only excuse is that this is the time when people who don't usually come to church, come to church; the Christmas crew. In ecclesiastical circles they are known as the fringe. They come at Easter sometimes as well. I was with them once: pile out of pub, pile into Midnight Mass, sing loudly and admire the blurred candles. The sermon was the boring bit, the part that had to be endured. I wasn't looking for God; I wanted my childhood, to see the breath pouring out of my mouth in the cold air, to hear the silence, to hear the silent things, to be earthed in angels. I wanted it to be the same as it always had been; the money went on the plate, that's what I was paying for, to take part in a performance. If the scenes altered, if the script changed, then the screen would tear to reveal reality and the magic was lost.

Heaven is a never-never land, Peter Pan is God. It's a wonderful place to be, this place where God does not grow up. As our society lets go of Jesus, God is becoming this rather ineffectual old magician who makes children laugh and flowers bloom. This person is incapable of dealing with earthquakes that kill thousands, the ethnic cleansing of villages in the Balkans, the greed of the Western world politely called progress. No, this God is incapable of defeating evil; we might like to think he can, she can, but we've all really been persuaded that it's simply not practical. Easter and Christmas have become the nice bit. As a man Christ was difficult, thank God; as a baby, wrapped in a clean towel, lying on straw he asks us kinder questions, perhaps.

Jake was in church yesterday for the first time since his accident; he was involved in a head-on collision while on business in Europe. He's in a wheelchair now. It was lovely to see him. He has an open face. The Christingle service seemed to go quite well; the beautiful small church in Harlton was just about full, children making a noise; our Sunday services are usually very quiet, very prayerful. At this time of year the sun is low in the sky – it comes through the windows, cracked through the shadows of the rookery trees, it lights the whole place. It's very, very cold. There are some alien-shaped heaters that light up on four sides three metres off the ground; they heat the roof and little else. There's a big funeral there on Tuesday. Matt died very suddenly last week. He was a popular man for good reasons.

There's a traveller sleeping in the porch of Haslingfield Church. He told me his boots had satellite markers in them so 'they' knew where he was. He said he'd come from the surgery in Harston; he asked them about voluntary euthanasia which by all accounts they found more frightening than he did. It's horrible judging people but you have to. I offered him a meal but he said he never ate anything that other people had cooked – it played havoc with his digestion. His favourite biscuits were Rich Teas, he ate whole packets of them while we were talking. I hope he's there tomorrow morning. I've given him the key; he's going to leave it in an old traffic cone. There's nothing quaint about being on the road; the air is bitter now. Once it reaches your bones it takes hours to get warm again. I admire travellers immensely. It is the hardest life – you suffer poverty and derision. People cross over the road when they see you coming. Mothers pull their children towards them. Only Rod chose to live that way – the rest, the ones I'd met, have all had to. Perhaps that was the purpose of priests – it was definitely the purpose of prophets – to live on the outside of the culture, to live with God. To breathe God. Perhaps that is what 'following God', 'following Christ' is all about. I follow a script you see, I've been trained to. The years are ordered into 'one' and 'two' parts, the Sundays have names like Epiphany 3 and Pentecost 14. The readings are all laid out. The services are written. I have taken vows to visit the sick, to marry people, to bury people, to obey the bishop. There's nothing wrong with any of it; it's surely the spirit that it's done in that matters most, and in a true Christian tradition you could claim that it was all a discipline, a method to lead you into the arms of God. I haven't stopped loving God because of it. I am rescued continually from it by the God that speaks through all of us, by the struggle we all go through to overcome disappointment and shame with love, the struggle to choose love above all the other distractions that insist on being heard.

I believe now that truly to follow God, quite literally, means that some of us may want to give up what we have and take to the roads, sleep in what's left of the hedges, freeze in February, burn in July. It's not so ridiculous. I will do it one day. I've wanted to do it; I wanted to do it as part of the time I was a curate. The Bishop of Huntingdon agreed, most of all he didn't seem at all shocked. It was my wife who pointed out to me that as I had grown up without a father did I really feel that it was a good thing even for nine months, and secondly that my responsibilities lay with the children. She was right, of course; we agreed that it would have to wait. But there is a tension, a huge tension between this wild and intimate source of the universe of life, of love and the possibilities that that presents, and the way in which the church expresses those possibilities. If there is a moral malaise in this country, in the West, the church is surely part of it; we have blessed it all, you see, and the way things are currently structured we have been ransomed by it. We are imprisoned in it. I agree with the vitriolic piece in the *Independent* the other day: the church has too many official privileges and institutional perks; we've effectively been ransomed by them, held in check. We are protected by the Crown; that used to be worth something, I'm sure.

There have been two funerals this week, both very different. Yesterday there was standing room only in Harlton Church for Matt. The day before there must have been barely ten of us at the crematorium. Winter is a busy time for undertakers, it's the dying time; more people die in winter than at any other time of the year. In that sense it is kind. I'm not mad on crematoria, death made neutral. The crematorium in Cambridge is just off the busy A14. They are not places to go back to if you can help it. They are places no one wants to remember, a cross between a doctor's waiting room and the social security office.

We have pulled death to the edges of society. Mortality has become a bit of an embarrassment really; it is untidy and dirty and reveals all our weaknesses at once. It makes lepers of lovers, perhaps it always has done. Unless we go to God we end up with the worms. Tombstones have changed dramatically over the last fifty years: the sentence of scripture, the references to God are in the minority and falling fast. Most people still believe in an afterlife, they just happen not to choose to express that belief in the form or corporate style of the Church of England. The lichen is devouring its memory. 'The Lord is my Shepherd' might still have some cultural resonance in New Zealand or Morocco, but here it is at best poetry that needs understanding and at worst quaint nonsense. Jesus' parables are the same; they are earthed in the fields, dripping off the ears of wheat, there with the sheep, goats, chickens. This was a man who drew heavily on the world he saw and the way in which that world was expressed. You won't find the prodigal son today on a pig farm; you'll find him mainlining Horse in the back streets or up in the smashed-lightbulb floors of tower blocks.

There's a lot of chat about how the church needs to engage contemporary culture; the fact that it's taking place at all means we have fundamentally failed to engage contemporary culture. The main problem is that no one is asking why. There are no mistakes in the Church of England; individually we make mistakes, individually we make very big mistakes, but there is no blame, no one is accountable for the past. As far as I can make out we haven't had a bad day since the Reformation. It was the rise of youth culture in the sixties, free love, marijuana, the phenomenal festivals that really revealed just how self-important, just how pompous, just how wooden and moribund the church had become. When John Lennon said that the Beatles were bigger than Jesus everyone got very huffy, the church stamped its feet like a spoilt child, a few records were burnt, but he was right. He was expressing really the end of the age of deference, he knew it; it was the end of the age when police constables and headmistresses and the foremen of the works put on their best and did their duty by going to church. It wasn't just the hippies that dropped out in the sixties, they dropped out too from the church and we haven't seen them since. Sixteenth-century English was no match for Ziggy Stardust. This should have been a religious experience: we never had a divine right to be right. We have no divine rights at all, thank God. It was a combination of self-importance, self-centredness and self-indulgence, all steeped in a sycophantic culture that sidelines its prophets and is being crushed under the weight of its own traditions.

When I was a curate the vicar and I struck a deal. Whenever the press turned up to photograph us together with a group of people we would always be looking into the sky. I wish we'd kept the press cuttings. A lady from the chapel said that all church communities have an AB; I think she meant an awkward brother. Despite the fact that it's a little sexist, as things currently stand she's right. They're also worth their weight in gold because they are prepared to disagree and put everyone's backs up in the process. Although they can make life very difficult, they are invaluable because they embody the unpopular viewpoint. It would be worse than awful if we all sat around and agreed with each other. They are the cloves of this world. You wouldn't want to eat a whole one but the dish simply wouldn't have as much flavour without them.

It's very cold now, ice on the windscreen. Every Thursday the Readers and some vicars meet in Toft Church. We sat there with our collars high, the blood drained from our faces. The psalms turned the air to dust that lit up then disappeared into the sunlight.

I do love this – praying becomes an even greater mystery. It doesn't matter that it's cold. God speaks in truth, the truth about you. It is a voice and a sense and a feeling but, most of all, it is knowing without understanding where the knowledge came from. It is a hearing when the only discernible sound is silence. There is a discipline to prayer – sitting still or kneeling. I'm not sure that it's necessary, it's just something we learn; it becomes a habit, that's all. Prayer is a gift given by God to human beings; it is translated, transmuted through us and we hand it on to the world around us. It was us who fell in the Garden of Eden, not creation. It was not the apple's fault that Eve picked it, Adam ate it.

The crucifixions that humanity imposes on creation are brutal and endless; we are the poison in the air, it is our teeth in the traps, our misery in the crammed battery cages and concrete piggeries. We have such a low view of our own dying flesh and we have inflicted it on everything we eat; we displace, we eradicate.

This has all been couched so sweetly in a view of animals

as entertainers, the wonder of it all that conveniently hides the fact that we are killing all of it. These programmes on the environment, on nature, make us feel better but they are in danger of bequeathing to us no more than a global zoo, controlled and managed zones where wildlife is permitted. We're probably there already. This isn't living in harmony, this isn't celebrating creation; it is subjugating it, defeating it, living apart from it, not with it.

I go up to the mountains sometimes. They terrify me, some of them. All my fear, my fragile bravery is overcome, I have been close to my limits. But you will not find God unless you are prepared to climb. It's no good sitting at the bottom and saying it's a mirage, the mountain is for fools and that you believe it's there – but climbed or unclimbed it makes no difference. You can still have the mountain without ever climbing it. But you will never know it's real, you will never see how it might make you feel, unless you try. You'll be dependent on everyone else's words, not your own.

My youngest son has taken to ambushing me. He stalks me round the house Kato-style from the *Pink Panther* films. Yesterday we thought we'd lost him. We were in the no-man's-land between sanity and panic when he jumped out from under a beanbag which I must have walked around and over at least twenty times. 'I'm Peter Pan, you are stupid, Captain Hook!' He was right, of course. This morning Peter Pan spent most of his time in the pulpit waving with great amusement to the hundred or so people beneath it. My wife finally gave up after my sermon. It was just after our youngest daughter had fallen off the steps and banged her head on a pew. The howling that followed drowned the PA completely. So they came home.

When all the lights were out and the candles were on at the

Christingle service in Haslingfield you couldn't actually see the oranges and the cocktail sticks. There was something about it. There was a sense of God who, at these services, is more often than not described as magical or knowing or calming. It was all of those things and much more. I would still be happier, though, simply having the candles and doing away with the oranges. A Midnight Mass for children; maybe we should move it to Christmas Eve next year and call it a candle service. Why should it be only adults who by virtue of the pub and their age experience the carols and the candlelight?

I have to take another funeral on Thursday. Thankfully I'm not expected at this one to talk about the lady who died last Wednesday. To be put upon by protocol, to stand up in front of a group of people you do not know and to be expected to describe the bones, the flesh and the heart of someone that they knew intimately is like being asked to walk on eggs. It's a ritual hung over from the time when most parishes had a vicar and most of the parish knew him. There is a time warp in operation here, where contemporary culture rather strangely expects the rigid format to operate at death and marriage. Since the rigid format is often cited as the *bête noire* of the church, by the public at least, this means you can end up taking part in a rather strange play of surreal contradictions at times. The coffin is marched down the aisle by the undertakers, done up in top hat and tails. Above the vicar reading 'Blessed are those who mourn, for they shall be comforted' are the strains of 'Strangers in the night', the organ version. The readings can range from 1 Corinthians to Zen and the art of climbing mountains. The vicar is then marched on to describe the person's life, some prayer follows and finally the curtains start to move to hide the coffin when we're hit with David Bowie's version of 'Sorrow'. Well, we're meeting at ten o'clock tomorrow to talk to the architect and the surveyor about the tower.

The meeting seemed to go well. There is a process here that I know nothing about whatsoever. None of us, apart from the architect or the quantity surveyor, have any experience in binding two sections of a fourteenth-century tower together. Priests have to be many things in varying measures. But we are increasingly hostages to the bricks and mortar – what should be really a very simple act of encouraging people to meet with God becomes complicated beyond all measure by the fact that the building happens to be falling down. I would imagine it is a far more romantic venture to build rather than to maintain. It's often said that faith has become much more about maintaining the buildings than the great silence of God. It is a parable in miniature in many ways: the church spends far too much time maintaining the church, maintaining its living rooms, not living with God. Yet in many rural areas churches are the only remaining icons of a community. The post offices have gone, the pubs have gone, and all that's left are these piles of medieval stones and the occasional flickering candle. The sense is there on *Dark Side of the Moon*, 'the tolling of the island bell, the softly spoken magic spell'. So much effort and time is spent reordering these buildings. I've been into churches that gleam with all mod cons but the air was empty, the atmosphere was centred on a kitchen and a toilet. The need for sanitation has sanitised everything. Hopefully a new generation will come along and take it all for granted. Thankfully new generations are really good at doing that. These buildings don't belong to us anyway; we are merely their guardians. We must surely pass them on to the next generation. In that sense it is deeply irresponsible to bequeath them a wreck, if only so that they should not have to worry about it, so that they are free to look for God on this journey that we so lightly call life.

It looks as if 'Public enemy number one' has been barred from church. I lost the debate in my absence. The alternative line which seems to have been given the nod is 'Meek. Mild. As if.' The visual of Christ in the manner of Che Guevara is thankfully the same. I don't like the line simply because there were times when Christ was meek. I see nothing wrong with being 'meek'. It also lacks the poise of 'Public enemy number one', which is what he became. The reality is, we're back on the fence again here, we're hedging our bets, we've taken out reassurance. The main argument apparently is that people over fifty do not understand 'Public enemy number one'. What's really being said is that they do not and cannot believe that Christ had more in common with Butch Cassidy and Robin Hood than he ever did with a civil servant or a king. He is portrayed as a king, we sing to a king, Christ the King, God the King; it is a perversion of both history and faith, a line carved on crowns. It stakes a claim to authority and power using the language of an institution that has neither. It might have been convenient to give God a crown but God looks like a playing card wearing it now.

Too often we end up, for the sake of politics and pleasantries, compromising the truth we are charged to represent. We spend too much time turning wine into water. Everyone knows priests believe in Jesus, believe in God, but it is how we represent that belief that is critical: how we paint it, sing it, sew it, write it. All priests have been transformed: we have shed a skin and taken on another one. The tension between the institution of the church and God is enormous, dreadful.

It's been almost warm; there was a rich storm last night. The trees turned to water, the branches of the holm oak in the garden rushing together, the leaves brushing and breaking, mimicking the sound of the sea – it was wonderful to watch. President Clinton has been impeached while American and British planes bomb Baghdad. Violence and sex together, the media are in a dream. Saddam Hussein appeared on a pre-recorded video using the language of God, and the American President, we are told, was in prayer during the impeachment proceedings. There they met, perhaps.

Christmas doesn't appear to have been a mad juggling festival this year. The phone hasn't rung that much either. Usually if I step out for a couple of minutes, by the time I return there are nine messages on the answerphone. But no one is calling. It is silent, it is as silent as snow. The reason for this is that I'm very busy. That's the official line – maybe I should be, but I'm not. I have to write four sermons and visit as many people as I can, but I'm not inventing machinery, it's all there. I can't remember ever enjoying a Christmas so much. David Jenkins, the former Bishop of Durham, has my vote on the nativity stakes, the questions he asks about the wise men and the virgin birth, but it is amazing – you do turn more compassionate at Christmas; we allow God to the surface of our time. The wooden perception, the modern perception, is perhaps to forget it all for a day. I wouldn't call it a forgetting; it's more a remembering perhaps, a remembering of God, God with us: the great incomprehensible scenery that is celebrated by the carols. It is actually very embarrassing that this man was born in a stable. Anyone who has seen a human being delivered into this world has met that miracle, can see that it is not this sanitised picture-perfect glitter-filtered arrival that the fairy tale tells us it is. This was a first-time mother giving birth on an earth floor. It is actually more extraordinary for it.

Well it's nearly all done; there's one sermon left. It's rained all day, everything is sodden, the wind has gone. There was fog this morning. It obliterated the distance; we woke up in a box without sides.

Four boys have been excluded from the local school; a quarter-ounce of cannabis passed through various hands and corridors. The families are devastated. I saw two of the boys last night, young confused faces, so clear and clean. I'm not under any illusions about teenagers and their experiments with adult pleasure, their certainty that beauty and music hold the keys to eternal life. When you have both of those it may feel that way. But their punishment has more to do with league tables and reputation than reality. What kind of world is it where an adult who's busted for possession for two ounces of cannabis is more than likely in the current scheme of things to get no more than a caution? They don't lose their job and it doesn't have to be public knowledge either. It seems grossly unfair that a fourteen-year-old should be treated in such a way that bears no resemblance to adult life or reality. Adult hands are washed in public of their fate. It is no way to bequeath trust and understanding; they become someone else's pieces to be picked up elsewhere.

The school carol service was a performance for the parents really. We had the orchestra and the nativity, and the whole forty-five minutes was in aid of the housing charity Shelter. We were led down some dark alleys and into some bedsits where the paint was peeling. Santa could have burst in at any moment. The government has made it very difficult here. This is, of course, religious education steeped in a cocktail of ritual and history, spliced with the social issues of our time. The syllabus decrees that all religions should be taught – that's fine. But it is perhaps part of the same mindset that forced Christianity down children's throats which quite understandably left most of them spitting it out as quickly as possible. Why enforce one religion when you can enforce all of them? It also means that schools are free from having to make a decision; they can appeal to as many people as possible without offending anyone, except our friends the fundamentalists. The result is an insipid social soup which tastes of nothing in particular but leaves an uncomfortable feeling of having been squeezed into a box to be ticked. We are left with a manual to world religion. I'm not saying we should go back to enforcing Christianity; that experiment has thankfully failed. But I would rather it was something rather than nothing – that we taught our children about love and justice, sacrifice and peace, rather than the colour of cassocks, a Ramadan menu or a Hindu dance. None of these would come into being without prayer.

Tippex has escaped. He has Houdini in him, a white flash of a hamster. It's the fourth time he's managed it. His previous excursion lasted for a week somewhere in the ceiling between the bathroom and the loo. Jacs had several sleepless nights – she was certain that, out of pure hunger, he would start to eat the electric cable, short-circuiting the entire house, which would lead to the one spark that set the whole place on fire. At least we could hear him that time, scuttling around under the floorboards, but at the moment it's all gone horribly quiet.

I've been to the pub. I had a couple of pints in Harlton at the Hare and Hounds, which were both bought for me, and then on to the Little Rose, Haslingfield, which was fantastic, vibrating with the Verve and the catch-all Christmas album: John Lennon,

Slade, Wham, 'Last Christmas I gave you my heart, but the very next day you gave it away.' This is a Babysham Christmas, all the trimmings without the turkey, Bacchus in full flow. It is a pagan feast, the rituals are very different. Midnight Mass starts in forty-five minutes. I've been told one hundred times today that Christmas is for children. It's a dreadful let-out; it excuses adults completely from it. It is a time perhaps when we become like children. Is that so bad? It's a time when we are allowed to wonder. No wonder the Christmas cards take us back to the past. We are not hit with scenes of Oxford Street crushed to the corners; the toys are all wooden. It's innocence that we buy, a past innocence that we are all part of, or so we think: the time when we believed in Santa Claus and the lights on the tree were made of magic, Angel Gabriel was unchallenged, the carols sounded so sweet. We go to desperate lengths to recreate that holy day, that holiday. The story is the same – it's the same for a child as for an adult. You can believe it if you want to, believe it happened. God does not seek to control us.

It's Christmas Day. It's raining now, wonderful water coming in on the wind. Our children are in bed. They were up at around five, they fell asleep this evening with the safe sound of the rain on the windows. Every year I say the same thing, try to boringly instil some order into the present-opening bit. The order lasts for about one round; I lose control completely after they have gone round the circuit a couple of times. By that time the whole thing has developed its own momentum as hands, paper, sweets, cars, dolls, books and swords appear out of nowhere. Then they all take off their clothes and try on new Star Wars underpants, fairy dresses and fake leopard-skin trousers. I have a vague memory of this from my childhood. My grandmother, who came to live with us after my father died, used to hit the Babysham pretty hard over lunch. She would then set about clearing up all the pieces of paper. She would pick them up in huge scoops and take them outside and burn the whole lot. There was one Christmas when she also torched my sister's brand-new pair of white tights in the process.

The services were somehow very formal this morning. The conclusion is that going to church is stuffy and dull – it can be. But perhaps it's an honest attempt to settle people's hearts. The trouble is that as priests we get used to it, we get drawn into the order, it becomes a meditation in itself. It is actually different every time; the words come at you as they are, with what you have actually brought to bear on them; they are never dull. We learn to worship between the lines, through the lines, until it all becomes necessary and we tie God into it and form committees to change words, because we don't want to be upset. We have this great Protestant legacy, these expanses of freedom under God, and yet we impose order. I saw Bernstein conducting in a documentary: he jumped and he swayed, he cried and laughed. He took part and was part of it at the same time. He wasn't the distant conductor. He wasn't separate or elevated from the purposes of the music; he was in the music, was the music.

The birds are playing out the day, the sky is the colour of smoke, the colours of the sunset have gone. It's a robin, I think. There's one now that comes into the shed and waits outside by the back door in the morning for food. Last May I had the door open and a swallow dived in. I wish it had nested. It was looking for a suitable site to glue their mud together.

The carol service was mad. I was accosted at the door as everybody came out: 'That was rubbish and I won't be coming again.' Apparently their opinion is the popular vote. The trouble was we didn't line it with well-known carols; there were two or three of them out of the seven, that's all. The others were not obscure; they were just from the B list. We were expected, I'd been told, to lay on the traditional carol service. This is what the twenty-four-year-old who complained to me wanted. She doesn't usually go to church, but when she does come she obviously expects certain things. There's a creeping contradiction going on here. She would judge the church to be self-serving and out of touch, and yet she wanted the very performance that keeps it in that box. She wanted tradition with all the trimmings, and yet for the other 364 days I had no doubt the church would take a great deal on the chin for being tied in tradition. What's more disturbing is the fact that God was obviously there in the Christmas cards – one reinforces the other.

The Dean of King's College, Cambridge, says theology is dead. It has been strangled by its own tenuous threads, the high-wire act is over. The legacy of legions of academics all trying to answer their own questions has left the church stranded on the end of a blunt pin.

The massive failing of theology has been to make the food of faith indigestible to most people in this country. The hard currency of theology can only be exchanged between a few sincere and learned souls sitting in a few learned chairs. What have they honestly done for the church? Do we really need another book on the resurrection, another book on St Paul's letters to the Corinthians – as fascinating as these things may be – and who in the pub really gives a flying fig whether John's Gospel came before Mark's? They talked in the late seventies about the Labour Party being consciously manipulated and used by a small bunch of militants for their own ends. The same has happened to the church; it has fallen into the hands of professors and doctors of divinity. They have been busy entertaining each other while the fabric of the institution crumbles around them. No wonder no one can hear us; we spend most of our breath talking to ourselves. No wonder people do not understand what we are going on about; it is for the most part a private conversation that has failed to communicate its wonder and purpose beyond the High Table it has elected to sit at.

We can see the architect's dreams, they go on around us; the two fat ladies can transform a lettuce into something delectable before our eyes; Damien Hurst shocks us, John Tavener stills us, Paul Scholes can entrance us: there is an end in all of these. Yes, there is romance in the infinite and the stunning sands of our souls, but have we not made God unimaginable, bound him, bound her, in books? Maybe for all its endless words one or two drip through. Christ did teach theology, but without the action of love theology disintegrates into theory, becomes dead skin, castles cold as pills; theology without love has nothing within it. The current training system tends to train theologians; it does not train priests. Endless lectures using trees and trees of words on paper, history, communion, liturgy, Matthew, Genesis, on and on. The public don't give a toss about theology. Why should they? It doesn't speak to them, it hasn't died for them, theology never made sense of God. Very rarely does it come down from the high tables and mix in with the rest of us. *Honest to God* was probably the last book to cross the fence between the church and society. In this vacuum has burgeoned the New Age movement, crystals, auras, healing through touch, tarot, the zodiac. What sticks in my throat is that all this and more is chastised by the church, but we are largely responsible for its popularity. Where are the priests? Where are they? The priests of the alleys, the priests of the birds, the priests of the addicts, the priests of the alpha, the omega, the priests of the thin places? The church has, for the most part, become a society of intellectuals exchanging papers. There is nothing wrong with knowledge; it is, however, what you do with it that matters. Theology is a rich food, but by the time it hits the streets it is cold, it has sapped our energy. For the most part we stand in cold palaces, there are too many cold faces. We have made God cold, cold and old.

Our youngest son is not well; he's asthmatic, he has a virus. He's used to suffering; he's suffered most over the last three years. His eyes are gummed up with conjunctivitis and his chest rattles. Moving doesn't help, moving around I mean, changing climates. We've moved three times in four and a half years, it's all part of it: theology college, a curacy up on the wild, wild Fens and now here back to Cambridge again. You lose a sense of place and a sense of intimacy that goes with knowing the graffiti, the way a hedgerow has tangled itself together over the years, you lose the leaves. We have been outsiders in all these places. Not owning anything is liberating because it simply reinforces the reality that it's a nonsense anyway. We can paint the walls purple and, yes, we can own the bricks, the wiring, the tiles and the plaster, if it makes you feel better. You can fall in love with it all if you want to, but it doesn't make it yours. It's a joke really, the Van Gogh flowers sold for what, £24 million? They belong to Van Gogh, they can never belong to anyone else. We are just tenants, all of us; we're only here for a short time. The temptation is to leave our litter for the next generation to pick up. There is the ghost of nuclear energy and more besides; the world is surely remodelled, remade by each generation. It appears constant. We look at history as a practical stream of events culminating in this second – maybe it's easier to take it all in that way. We can only dream of what life was like before sherbet fountains and chicken tikka masala. We can never know.

Maybe our ancestors all struggled for peace, craved it. We've rather given up on it: peace belongs to politicians and soldiers, the peace movement. It's become grand, it's there in the passing of pens between one leader and another. We have accepted that our life is hard and that the struggle is actually what makes us. The peace of God, God's peace, the sense of peace realised in experience and the presence of God, is extraordinary. It's extraordinary because you experience it at the very core of your being, it is both eternal and internal, vast and intimate to each and every atom at the same time. An atom is a curious thing really, the great stillness of the nucleus and the unending movement of the electrons around it. When that tension is forcibly broken by us for our own ends all hell breaks loose.

Satan – or is it fear? – would have us disturbed, agitated, unable to settle, would have us sell ourselves into ambition in the empty alleyways of bigger things. There is so much theology about the femininity of God and yet Satan remains doggedly male – he has a masculine mask at any rate. The victims of the Protestant work ethic are undoubtedly legions upon legions of Protestants who would rather be busy than anything else, buying and selling each other and the rest of us. Human living is crushing human being – there is no profit in inner peace, so perhaps it is not necessary? The peace that passes all understanding is beyond description, beyond buying. Christ was right: it actually involves a reorientation of what you are focusing on, the stones you place under your feet. How long can you stand silence? Is keeping your face worth more than losing it? Peace, peace be with you, peace.

January

We had a few people over for a glass of something on New Year's Day. I can't say a lot of alcohol was consumed. The rural dean, who stands at about six foot three, took a lot of frustration out on a very large Bloody Mary, but most people stuck to white wine. It must be the only party we've ever had where we actually ended up with more alcohol than we started with. People were very generous and brought bottles – most of them weren't drunk at all. The two churchwardens from Haslingfield came. Sarah was an angel in a former life. She has the face of the good fairy in the Wizard of Oz, the woman in the white dress who appears to make snow and again at the end, I think, to tell Dorothy that all she had to do to get home was click her heels together three times. Anyway, she's retired now and masquerading as Sarah. Edward is as solid as an English oak, matured in Chateauneuf-du-Pape. He was made for Christmas; he is as warm as a log fire. It would be impossible to do the job without them. Sarah is training to become what is rather confusingly called a Reader. This means that she will be able to take funerals and baptisms and preach as well. She will be a far better priest than I ever will be. The role of the churchwarden has changed – it's now more pastoral than civic, which is a very good thing. With four parishes my role is far too civic. Maybe all it needs is time, the time it takes real relationships to form. This will evolve, I hope, into something more pastoral. Well, it's 1999. The bellringers rang in the New Year; it was a loud and uncompromising clamour swelling the gentle stars. There were rockets going off somewhere. The place to be next year would be on top of the hill. If it's a still night the sound of every bell and cheer would be extraordinary.

London this morning was almost quiet. I walked from Green Park to Methodist Central Hall. The coots called out on the lake in St James' Park and the pelicans looked ridiculous. In the winter you get the roofs through the trees that are crushed onto the reflection in the water; they made the sky look brown. Methodist Central Hall is a cross between the Natural History Museum and a Doctor Who set. It doesn't bustle, the dust stays in the corners, it's overwhelmingly grey, and there is the feeling that you could be set upon by a Dalek at any moment and this wouldn't be at all out of the ordinary.

The launch was at eleven. There must have been about twenty journalists there and we talked for about an hour. We showed the poster; Jesus stared at all of them. How he will appear in tomorrow's papers I don't know. Ruth Gledhill from the *Times* asked the most difficult questions. The *Daily Mail* will tear it to pieces. The journalist asked how we felt about Volkswagen cars using Nazi imagery to advertise their latest model, so it doesn't bode well on that front. I suppose we were too close to it really; it's difficult not to be. The blond-haired Jesus standing in an ivy-covered doorway holding a lamp, the stained-glass Jesus of centre-stage, this sweet Jesus, this comfortable Jesus, was not on offer here. He didn't end up being crucified for being kind, not really. He was crucified because he was dangerous, he was a threat. That doesn't mean we have to be, or should be. But without that piece of the puzzle it's easy to slip into soft focus, you end up with a gentle man who was wrongly crucified. It almost gets to the point where you feel sorry for him. No, that's not the man we are dealing with here. He did cause a revolution, a revolution in the way we absorb and recognise love, a revolution in the way we interpret love, a revolution in the way we respond to suffering. He displaced an autocratic distant deity with an intimate loving Father: the Holy Spirit speaks in those terms. No wonder people who hear it die for it. It reveals the beauty in all of us, in all of you.

It started yesterday evening with the *Birmingham Evening Post* leading on the front page with 'Unholy Row'; there was, in fact, no row at all. The *Telegraph* rather predictably dived in this morning with 'Church Poster Shows Jesus as Che Guevara' in relation to the headline 'Meek. Mild. As If.' The Bishop of St Albans said that young people might think that As If was a pop group. How he reached that point we will never know. The *Independent* was keen to assure its readers that the posters were condemned as grossly sacrilegious by Harry Green, the former Tory MP who sponsors the Conservative Christian Fellowship. He went on to say, 'I feel extremely strongly about this, and those who are in any way responsible should be excommunicated.' The *Times* coverage was very fair and well written, but the *Daily Mail* really went looking for trouble, trumpeting blasphemy: 'Che shot wavering comrades, he was responsible for hundreds of executions.' In all of this, every paper has failed to mention that it is not the image of Che Guevara; it is clearly the image of Christ.

By this evening this was the campaign that no one has yet seen except via the newspapers, and it was the campaign that was causing outrage on Anglia Television which went on to say that the people who produced it were not prepared to back down. Where did that one come from? So far there has only been outrage from one ex-Conservative MP – is that enough outrage to become plural? No, it's enough outrage to become puerile and no more. Ann Widdecombe has been the only person to come back with sharp, powerful and incise criticism; she was quoted in the *Guardian* as saying 'As far as this poster goes we should be modelling ourselves on Christ, not modelling Christ on us.' I agree entirely. But we cannot have a sanitised Victorian version of the story. Christ was not forcibly arrested in Gethsemane for smiling, he *was* Public Enemy Number One. Yes, the revolution he inspired was based on love, based on peace, but it was a revolution nonetheless. It may be very uncomfortable for the Establishment to be reminded that part of this narrative involves a man who was on the run, a man who was viewed and crucified as a religious outlaw. Clearly the tension between the reality that led to his death and the way we celebrate his resurrection is enormous; they are two sides, however, of the same story. The reality of Christ is surely weakened if we ignore either of them.

The press cannot have it both ways: they cannot shout at the church for staying in the box and shout at us when we attempt to climb out of it. As the art director of the posters so eloquently said, 'Those with the Sunday-school view of Christianity might be shocked by it, but anyone who reads the Bible regularly will not be.' Maybe that's the problem we need to address. Our intention was not to shock and not to offend, it was to inform. I'm only sorry that this appears to be yet more petrol poured on the pews. We clearly portrayed revolution in a one-dimensional way and Christ's revolution was very different from the revolution practised by Che Guevara. We are not saying that these methods were the same, we are simply taking an icon of revolution and saying first of all, think about what revolution is, what it achieves, and secondly that there is a great deal more to be explored about the persona and image of Christ than the traditional Victorian and renaissance imagery allows. It's time we moved on.

The Canadian Broadcasting Corporation kicked off at six o'clock in the morning. The main South African radio station is calling to discuss the ad and on Monday there's an interview with a German television station. This poster seems to have set fire to something. The *Independent* this morning had Tom Ambrose and me cast as the reverend revolutionaries: 'In the beginning the brief was with God and the brief was God.' I have finally reached the conclusion that there is a massive tension between the church as part of the Establishment and Christ who clearly wasn't. Maybe this explains the almost neutral images, the sweet Victorian portraits which cast Christ in clean clothes with a face the colour of sherry against a backdrop of saccharine landscapes. These images are very powerful, though, and there has been nothing contemporary to replace them. As a consequence Christ is conveniently cast in the past. He is treated by the public as a historical figure, not as a contemporary.

I'm not generally anti-theology – it is the meat of our faith – but it has rendered the church pretty useless at the point where it meets the world. I'm sure that's been very convenient, but roses have thorns; they are surely the more beautiful because of them.

The children were all expelled, all four of them, four lives will carry that with them for ever now. It's called permanent exclusion. What a ludicrous system: it just means the school doesn't have to deal with it. It becomes someone else's problem, a victory of public relations over private knowledge. Fourteen is still very young to experience the foul taste of injustice and you are at that age completely powerless to fight it. Maybe these boys will take it in, maybe whenever they encounter injustice in the future they will stand up against it, or maybe they will just accept that it is part of our world. If they do that then it is quite understandable that it all becomes worth a good deal less than it was before. But what are we teaching them here, by pushing their secrets into the shadows? Are we not teaching them to be deceitful, to lie? If as adults we can't bear it, can't deal with it, what does this say to children? Tomorrow is Sunday; I hope Sarah is saying the prayers.

It was football tonight, the crowning glory on a mad day. It's vanity really, chasing this round bouncing object around an indoor arena. I'm now at the point where it takes me nearly all week to recover from the game itself, as the cells inside take longer to replace themselves, the bruises last, the limping lingers. It might be worth it if I was in any way competent. I was in here at eight planning a service with the chapel on Sunday. This need for ecumenism – it's a great theory, but in practice it simply means more work. The truth of it is that we are in competition. The chapel is warmer than the church – it's a modern building with a lino floor. It doesn't have the frills, the quaint dust and the cracked lead of Haslingfield. But does that matter? Perhaps to old souls or passionate fools. At the mid-week communion this morning everyone was wrapped up, advertising each breath. It's not a chore at all, it's a time to be with God. It is space in between the phone and the endless papers and planning.

This afternoon we entertained the Diocesan Advisor on architecture. Every brick, every act of each builder's finger has to be agreed in the name of preservation, in the name of history, in the name of responsibility. You can't just go funky and paint the pillars purple; everything has to be done in the best possible taste. It's almost impossible to change a light bulb without a piece of paper – it *is* impossible to change a light fitting without one. The weight of history is dreadful, churches which must have evolved extreme architectural exuberance in their time are now confined by the same pen that drew them. Why are we propping up history and enshrining fourteenth-century architectural quirks. Why is the past more precious than the present? I'd really like to put some wild sofas in, have an area where people could simply relax. They are not relaxing places, are they, really. They're hard, the wood is hard, the walls are huge and cold, they are terribly austere, a concentration of death usually, not life. Harlton has this plaque which records the death of six children. There is also a huge marble monument which arrogantly takes up half a window. It appears on the front of the odd church journal. It's so kitsch, it's fantastic.

The architect who is overseeing the tower restoration of Haslingfield has the most amazing gift of being able to talk for fifteen minutes, without, it appears, needing to breathe. He has a face that was drawn in the *Pickwick Papers*. We are at his mercy – none of us has any experience of binding one piece of the church tower to another. All we can hope for is that contemporary restoration techniques will have a longer credibility lifespan than the Spice Girls and that our grandchildren won't curse us for filling in the holes in a way we feel confident will solve the problem. We can only do our best and hope that fifty years from now the process does not have to be repeated. But as a process it is enshrined in conservatism. The Victorians did some pretty awful things inside churches. But at least they did them; there was obviously a confidence there that we do not possess, it does not possess us. I love old churches – the timeless light and the sweet songs they sing, the children that run unencumbered, released into space. Have you noticed how they choose to whisper?

The rain has finally gone. It seems to have washed some of the blue from the sky. You know how in summer there is that deep luminous blue that makes the planes seem silver? The millennium is firmly on the agenda, that and the computer. The official, non-instructive-guide-sort-of-suggestion leaflet is trying to encourage services at midday on 1 January 2000. The logic for this seems hewn out of fantasy. I would imagine there will be some hangovers of the millennium to contend with. The planners of these services have somehow missed this, or will it be that all Christians will go to bed with a cup of cocoa at 10 past 12? In Harlton one of the farmers is kindly holding a dance in the barn, which is due to last until whenever. The PCC decided to walk the couple of hundred yards up to the church and wait for the bells in there. We are planning to do the same in Haslingfield. Jacs and I are going to wake up our children and take them up. Whether they will go back to bed after that remains to be seen.

The diocese are very keen for all incumbents to go on line with an email address and all the rest of it, parishes are being asked to foot the bill for the connection. We have one computer but it's for our children, so I suggested that all three parishes club together and buy a computer which will then be passed on to the next vicar here. The poster still seems to be burning on. It was in the *Daily Mirror* today, described as the church's brilliant new image. The *Evening Standard* the other day ran with the headline 'At last a Jesus that will scare the living God out of the Church of England. ' We have a word-based faith fenced in by theology; it's a private conversation. It's becoming quite clear that images of Christ are perhaps more sacred than he is, and that we have tampered with that. This notion of the sacred image was maybe what inspired Cromwell's foot soldiers to smash the statues and Roman Catholic glitter in our cathedrals and churches. By doing so they attempted two things. The first perhaps was to take ownership of the persona of Christ and to ensure the image they offered was, where possible, the only one available. Maybe they understood that the statues had become more potent than the person. This was their scourging of the temples. The churches may well have been Protestant, but Christ wore more Catholic clothes and there must have been a deep suspicion that he kept a Catholic heart.

The revolution poster is an outright challenge to those who own the image of Christ. It wasn't meant to be – it was simply meant to pose some questions to those who might consider looking for some answers. But it's gone way beyond that now. To simply say that image is unimportant and therefore we won't acknowledge its existence denies the fact that the church has an image, that Christ has an image. This is madness: the cross is the strongest logo the world has ever seen. Whenever we see the face of Christ, we tend to see this Western Renaissance man; the paint is cracked, the cross, according to image, went up in the fifteenth century. The Victorians threw in a bit of soft focus, but really it is the Sistine Christ that lives. Heaven is the same: huge scopes of rolling clouds and paint that's centuries old. There are no drugs in hell, no syringes, no electric torture, it's all very ball-and-chain-loaded with gothic gargoyles' faces, full of medieval monsters. No wonder people think it's a farce and that heaven is full of fruit and horses. The picture editor of the *Sunday Times* put up a painted frilly picture of Christ against a photograph of Che Guevara. As they rightly assumed, the first was the one we all know.

What does hell look like? What is heaven? I don't know and I agree the bliss of God is beyond all fashionable presumption and contains a promise far out beyond the limits of our imaginations, a world we can sense sometimes but not know, not yet. To that end it is unpaintable: it is a blue canvas, a red dot, a crash of colour, whatever. But to have Christ, heaven and hell portrayed as they are in the popular sense has made them historical icons – images that we can confidently ignore and assume are history. Some of the images may be worth a lot of money, but they are no more sacred than the graffiti in the belltower and, thankfully, a poster that was produced for Easter in 1995 or 1999 will be no more sacred than that either. They are all, however, trying to portray Christ in a way that resonates. They are the response of our imaginations to the questions of heaven and our natural curiosity as to what Christ did indeed look like.

It was just the one service this morning out at Great Eversden. Gordon, who is a non-stipendiary minister, has very kindly offered to take the services in Harlton and Haslinfield on the third Sunday of every month, which means I can go to the Eversdens. The organist bussed himself in from Cambridge; he had a child's face in a man's clothes. His skin was completely perfect; it was as if he had never been outside, never had a bruise, and had spent the last nineteen years reading books which he was a part of and playing music which he'd swallowed. He played everything at half-speed; that may sound strange but it suited the congregation. Then afterwards, after we had prayed and the hot chocolate came out of the packets at the back, he set off into these mesmeric chord sequences. Bagpipe players do it, I've seen them in their competitions. The aim isn't something to stamp to, the aim of the music is to be taken up by it and into it completely, so that you lose all sense of time and place – the music and the music maker is you. That is surely prayer. There can be no rational explanation for it; you can't teach it like maths. There's doubtless biology there – our brains are doing something, but it changes people's faces. I once saw a monk in St Benet's church in Cambridge: every line on his face was a prayer.

This evening we had the joint service at the chapel to kick off the week of Christian Unity. Last year I had flu and had completely forgotten about it; this didn't go down very well, understandably. The expectations on vicars are huge – there is a wood full of unwritten etiquette. We are not allowed to show anger and the mistakes we make are very grave because they always involve other people. There is a strict neutral dress code for men, very conservative shoes, with laces by and large, clean-shaven, no stubble, the occasional beard might be acceptable. You also have to relinquish your sexuality completely. You become almost totally sexless. Your sexuality is never mentioned, very rarely hinted at. It is simply rubbed out of the equation altogether. If I had no friends with complicated love lives, the only time sex would ever come up in conversation is when we preach that point in the marriage preparation, or the fact that I'd been kicked in the nuts playing football and had to ask the all-important question concerning my future prospects to my doctor. This is really a no-man's-land, a place where sex and sexuality do not exist. Clergy marriages as a result become very pressured, and in the absence of any kind of banter on the outside, of any kind of acceptance and recognition that to a heterosexual man, women's breasts and eyelashes and lips matter, it all becomes rather unreal. There's never one reason why a male vicar would choose to leave his family or be unfaithful. I can only say that we are very vulnerable on that front. For a vicar, simply to have your sexuality recognised by someone else, would be in itself a powerful experience, which is why perhaps with so much to lose – your family, your job, your house, everything – a fair proportion of clergy do take that road. It is also a different type of marriage. The space between the persona and the person can develop into an uncrossable desert. Partners are married to two very different people; they bear the full force of our sins, simply because it is impossible to express them without running great risks in any forum other than the four walls when no one else can see them; if they did you would be frogmarched out of the parish immediately. It's easy to become lost in the no-man's-land between persona and person, to compromise and to end up as too many people do, as neither. It is perhaps easier at the end of the day to be neither. But in a sense we're called into no-man's-land, called out of this world to be part of another world, there in the echoes.

February
· ·

Everyone is sick, all the children and Jacs. Harris had a temperature of 40.4 so we put him in the bath. He sat there hardly knowing us, his eyes lost; it was awful, he was so quiet. His temperature is down a bit now. People from the parishes have been very kind. Sarah came over with some food and offered to shop for us.

I had to go to London this morning for an Arbory Trust meeting, the group involved in woodland burial. Everything was wet. I wandered up Whitehall past the gates of Number 10. Tony Blair had just been dropped off with a crowd carrying briefcases. They looked small between the bars, dressed in Tuesday clothes. St Martin-in-the-Fields was more surreal than normal. Slap bang at the end of the aisle was a black grand piano. Playing it was a young Mediterranean-looking woman with eyes the colour of coal. Leaning up against it was a young man in a claret suit, an aquiline air; he was singing opera to the ten wayfarers sitting as far apart from each other as possible. He sang beautifully. It was a rehearsal for a concert at one. I can never walk past that church – I always go in. Twenty years ago I used to go for evensong. I don't know why, I only know that it was the only place where nothing was expected of me, that had no pressure to be anything, to say anything. There was a curate there called Andrew. Sometimes I would talk to him; once I went up to his study and we smoked cigarettes. I can't remember what we talked about.

I had been smoking too much cannabis before then. I would get up in the morning and roll a joint, and would repeat the process when it started to wear off. I used to buy it wrapped in silver foil from a squat on Elsham Road. The dealer was Brazilian. He would sit cross-legged in front of a huge window; there were orange sheets on the walls and he played a lot of Lou Reed. Sometimes I'd stay there all night. It was the women that fascinated me. I had no idea what they were saying, other than it was all in Portuguese. They would fly in and out – some of them would go through his sheepskin bag for money, sometimes they just danced. They were not interested in me, another young Englishman with bloodshot eyes. I was part of the carpet. It can screw you up, cannabis – it screwed me up. I was lucky to be rescued. The drug culture is very single-minded, very simple; it's all about drugs, what you take, what they do to you. Drugs kill your feelings first; if they can wipe them out your body becomes meaningless. If you cannot feel your heart, its existence is unimportant; whether it stops beating or not is immaterial.

The children seem to have turned the corner. Jonson is bouncing off the walls again, India is drawing, Eden is wearing other people's shoes once more. Harris is still unwell. He just lay down all morning, too weak to walk. He's a little better now. It's terrifying having children. I don't imagine it gets any better. Maybe when they have grey hair of their own, maybe then you can be slightly more sure that you will die before they will. Death registers make sobering reading – so many children used to die. I have not had to take a child's funeral yet. I would imagine it's like juggling with knives. We are all so protected in the West by antibiotics and clean hospitals. Too much of the southern hemisphere does not have these guarantees, children die all the time. I can only imagine the temptation to blame God must be overwhelming; it's a blueprint for bitterness though in the end.

Freedom cannot have any guarantees – there would otherwise be no freedom. Stephen Sykes, the Bishop of Ely, and the great Christian writer John Bowker part company here. The bishop says we are free, believes we are free. John Bowker takes the line that there are limits on this freedom and therefore we are not free; freedom is an illusion that we like to see. Are the secrets of God unknowable or is it that we simply do not know how to know them? Or could it be that they are unimportant?

This afternoon was down to assigning fees. Every time there is a funeral, a wedding, every time ashes are interred or a tombstone put up, there are charges. Some of the money goes to the church council and some to the diocese. Vicars don't get any of it – we are just a funnel that it passes through, that's all. They used to be given the collection on Easter Sunday morning, but this has largely been withdrawn now because any gift of this kind affects your tax code and it's simply not worth it. We are treated as a special case by the Inland Revenue. This is unfair, I grant you. There are tax allowances for the upkeep of the garden, and secretarial help. If there were not tax allowances, most vicars quite simply would go under; maybe this is part of the deal of being in the Establishment. We are, of course, in hock to it though, we have ended up pawning ourselves. I'm sure there is some delicate unravelling taking place – I hope so.

The new album by the Corrs is interesting. There are four

faces on the cover; what is it that makes a face beautiful? Sharon Corr stands out. How many people have made her, how many people have made you? We look at our parents and say it's them: no, there are many more; whose eyes and feet are entwined in our DNA? The German philosopher Hegel said we turn up in the middle of an unfinished story, with no knowledge of the past or future; we are essentially marooned. Maybe that was Nietzsche's pain, his awful end. Jim Morrison of the Doors said it more poetically: 'Into this house we're born, into this world we're thrown'; maybe Morrison was reading Hegel. Our spirits, our lost faces, they rattle around in search of God. The humanist would say we should give up this ancient nonsense, we are held back by these silver superstitions of a loving infinite being that surrounds us with angels no one can see, speaking in semiotics. The whispered words of tongues are distilled in a saliva of insanity. Prayer will not save us from our failings; belief and faith are insufficient words. They are the words people hear, they are the masks we wear. If we lived our faith, rather than thought it, they would not be necessary.

It was Sunday today. Haslingfield half past nine, Harlton eleven o'clock. Haslingfield still grates with politics. It's the one that gets turned over in the bath. Internal politics is crippling and totally against the concept of love and the service of others. Jockeying for position and influence; it stinks. As a vicar the worst temptation is to encourage a personality cult around yourself, to allow it air and food. It's easy to see the people that operate this way; they leave a parish with a well-publicised full church, which is near enough empty six months after they've moved on. Going to church is an individual choice; it should never be measured in individual gain.

Small Boat, Big Sea

It is the children and all their clatter that is saving Haslingfield. They are the happiest people there and thankfully it's proving infectious. The *Church Times* had another letter about the ad: 'Do the ad men want a revolution?' Mervyn Stockwood wrote it. I've heard his name mentioned deferentially. Does Tom Ambrose want revolution, does the Churches Advertising Network want revolution? We'd never discussed it. Do you want revolution, Mervyn Stockwood?

The couple who'd won each other in the radio competition were on television last night. They were on the news kissing in the hotel where they were married. They did look like the plastic couple on the wedding cake, albeit slightly bigger. This was a national story, it made the quirky spot at the end of News at Ten. This morning they were all over the front pages of the newspapers, free wedding photos for ever. I hope they will both want to remember it. Whether it will all work we don't know yet. The Western view of love is that it can't be arranged. Part of the chaos of teenage culture is teenage love which, so the theory goes, provides us with some sort of experience with which to choose a partner. In response to this national event the Church of England wheeled out that recognisable figure, the Archdeacon of Birmingham. He stood there in the regulation colourless anorak and issued the usual statement of shock and dismay. The managing director of the local radio station was next up, with the sobering statistics that only forty per cent of the population are bothering to get married, and forty per cent of those marriages are failing. If that is the case I find it slightly strange that he should want to make such a big deal out of this marriage or is this just the lion tamer throwing meat to the clowns?

The archdeacon, as the spokesman for marriage, was a complete disaster. He had about as much sparkle as a lump of mud and, as its official representative for the day, managed to imbibe the whole notion of spending the rest of your life with one person with the promise of limitless drudgery. The Church of England was the Patsy on parade, another ailing face worthy of a custard pie or two. On that performance we deserved a crowdful. Our response was on cue and on message; it was just what the media were looking for.

Anne invited me for lunch at my old theological college. The tables had moved in the dining room. They didn't run the length of the room any more – they'd been rearranged breadthways. Is this democracy at work? I hope so. The faces in the stained glass still looked as if they knew my most awful thoughts. One look from Martin Luther in the chapel still has the capacity to confirm my sinner-of-the-year status. He's right, of course. Anne has found a curacy in a thriving charismatically revived church; they are the future, the seed-beds of the future, the big urban and suburban set-ups with secretaries, youth workers, a band, lay preachers and a string of curates. The rural churches cannot compete with this focused ministry, the one-church wonder. In a village of 250 people there is simply not the critical mass you need to generate energy on that scale. To combine congregations might be the answer. But it is the fierce and stubborn loyalty of the village church congregations that is saving most of them.

The potency of a village church is, however, set to decline as most people quite naturally will vote with their feet and opt to attend churches that they like. The success of the one-church wonder is felt acutely here. Lots of people from these villages go into Cambridge on Sunday morning. There they can find a sung matins, an incense-filled Anglo-Catholic hour or two, a ferment of dedicated Evangelicals, Charismatics singing in tongues. The focus of ministry is changing; it is on the church, not the local population that surrounds it. The focus is on the style. It is the style that has become the benchmark, the measure of success, a church bustling with heat. We are creating *Quatermass*. Hot spots burn out on diocesan maps where the Holy Spirit is conducted through a magnifying glass and hits the paper, burning a hole in it. The area around it, however, remains cold. Ministry is focused inwards: the heat created may set Sundays on fire but, as is the case with so many urban churches, the petrol evaporates in the porch. I had friends living one street away from what was considered to be a highly successful model London church. They had no idea that it was taking on legendary significance. Maybe this is down to economics, economic reality which manifests itself in multi-parish benefices in the countryside and the drive-in churches of the city. I would imagine that most people drive to church in the cities now, and that more people drive to church in the cities now than they do in the countryside. The vicar serves the congregation, not the community. This isn't a criticism; it's a response to realism. Maybe they don't want bumbling beekeepers in Hammersmith. Haslingfield, Harlton and the Eversdens still want their vicar: they want the pastor, the tea drinker, the cricket player, they want their children married by someone who watched them grow up. The sense of disappointment when the vicar changes faces every week, when he or she trips up for an evensong once a month is tangible. The vicar is the minister everyone wants, but looking at any map of any diocese you can see the church can't afford them any more – they are becoming as much of a luxury as the scones we are meant to be eating. We have become cartoons, conforming to parody, smeared in journalistic ink, gagged by the secrets we keep.

The tension in Haslingfield is rising. I've been accused of only being interested in the young people, the newcomers, the back of the church. Sarah broke the news to me beautifully. I had heard it before; my response was that I wanted to try to foster an environment free of division, a place where we all focused on the grace and beauty of God, and that everybody was involved in that, young and old; that was essentially decisive in itself. The luxury of running a business is that if people consistently make it their business to undermine the management and morale, by making it quite clear that the person who's supposed to be responsible for it is a grade A git, then they're out: P45 on the desk and a believable list of excuses and they are gone. You can't do that in the church. It's a very good lesson indeed; you have to try to encourage those who are fundamentally opposed to you and to carry on suffering a little more quietly if at all possible. Since arriving in Haslingfield I have spent the majority of time fighting those who would far rather I wasn't actually here at all. I have to love them, but I don't have to like them, even though, being such a soppy git, I would love to like them, if only because it would make their lives and mine a lot happier. This all reached a sort of crisis point this morning when I broke down completely in the middle of the Eucharistic Prayer; there were these long silences as the tears thankfully won the battle over protocol during the main section of this long prayer. Tom came to the rescue and we eventually managed to struggle our way through the rest of it.

Change is an elixir for some and a poison for others. The trouble is you turn up as vicar in some place where you have no knowledge of the delicate strands that hold it together, no knowledge of what it is that binds the community together. You turn up with your own insecurities, your own obvious failings and you're expected to suffer those publicly and caress everyone else's quietly. There's nothing you can do except carry on. Being a complete tart who's paid to be the centre of attention, you might think, is exceedingly fortunate, but I'm not supposed to be doing this for me. Problems arise when I behave as if I am, and so they should: they are very valuable, your detractors.

I played football tonight like a three-legged dog, living off ever less glorious scraps. I always feel guilty about going. I'm out most evenings and voluntarily leaving the house again, simply so that I can pretend I can play football, is nothing other than selfish, really. I have condemned my wife to poverty; to add lonely evenings to that is not a good mixture. The pay-off for never being around in most middle-class households is a good holiday or two. My friends fly away to fantastic places with hot names; they always insist on paying for lunch, they bring food with them when they come and stay. Why people should want to stay in our house is still beyond me. We spend most of the night changing rooms. Harris and Jonson wake up at about half past five and the breezeblock walls cannot contain the gunfire that usually follows. By the standards of the Third World we are outrageously wealthy but we do not live in the third world and by the standards of this country we are not well off at all. Every week is a struggle and we are in deep debt. If it was just me I wouldn't be bothered by it, I really would be happy to eat dust. It's when other people are depending on you that it becomes critical. Being crap with money and mindlessly extravagant is probably at the root of it all – it makes our friend's chickens harder to swallow.

Glen Hoddle's gone. The media are taking no responsibility for it, the broadsheets seem to have been drinking with the tabloids – they all agree to agree. There hasn't been a witchhunt. These pipers charge too much for their tunes. Look back twenty years: Ron Greenwood hounded out, Gordon Taylor ridiculed, Bobby Robson treated viciously and disgracefully. Terry Venables was the only man who seemed to have the gift of putting his hand in the dog's mouth without being bitten. But it's a torrid record. I don't for one second share Glen Hoddle's theology, but we are surely approaching a dangerous whirlpool if a man can't say what he believes in without running the risk of being cut to pieces by it. It's all very well for sports journalists to go bashing on about the fact that he should have stuck to football; maybe they should have stuck to football too.

The fundraising meeting last night was the first of many: we're going to have to raise about £250,000 in Haslingfield. At the moment three out of the four churches either have building work taking place or it's just about to start. The fourth church has ruddy great cracks all over it and is probably in a worse state than the other three. All in all, to bring all the churches up to scratch, to provide sensible heating and see to the peeling paint and plaster, we're probably looking at around one and a half million pounds minimum. A very thorough list of jobs had been prepared for Haslingfield, which ran into three pages; that's probably one quarter of what needs doing and we're getting on with that this year. I would far rather be a vicar than a building projects overseer, but the reality is that over the next year at least the fundraising and all the other kerfuffle that goes with architects, faculties and quantity surveyors will, I think, account for half my time. Something has to give, it will probably be visiting. I love visiting, it's what matters in the countryside. When it doesn't happen you lose touch and the intimacy tends to crack a little.

Henry is dying now, he's had cancer ever since I've been here. When we arrived he was still walking to the shop, sometimes he would come to church in a brown tweed suit. He was a tall elegant man. His house is on the other side of the meadow. He was lying in bed sleeping, he's very thin; you do see people's secrets. I always thought that God would lose the gleam, that it would all slowly fade and become the colour of spilt tea. It doesn't – if anything the reality of God becomes more intense, there shining in people's eyes, slipping through your lips, the rooks singing their hymns. The sky was the colour of the road this afternoon. It soaked everything in a sullen gothic, hid Macbeth somewhere close. February in East Anglia belongs to the crows; they become conscious for twenty-eight days.

Henry died yesterday. He was fifty-nine. It was the first time I had ever seen him still. There is a very real sense that the person isn't there any more; maybe our bodies become too weak to contain us. It isn't like it is in the movies. Imagine how many deaths you've seen on film – we always see it happen, we don't see it half an hour later; when the baddies die the elation is switched on for us. The reality is far less colourful. It usually reminds you of some dangerous questions you would rather not answer. I have to believe that Christ is not being tortured by God on the cross. It is either the greatest piece of human folly ever, or the greatest demonstration of God's love. But if God is involved, it is not torture at all. Because of the cross Christianity is very accepting of pain, the pain that we all experience as part of being a human being. The celebration of this pain probably got a bit out of hand with orders of monks whipping themselves and maybe art is currently obsessed with the question, having done conventional beauty. The existence of pain cannot be merely written off as unjust. If we felt no pain we wouldn't feel anything else either. Yet sometimes it seems Western Christianity loves pain; perhaps it's all we think we have left. Why is the cross the supreme act of Christ? It was a supreme act, but by concentrating on it, all that Disney stained glass, we hold hands with a death cult. You always hear, don't you, 'Christ died for you.' Christ did die for you, but he also lived for you. He showed us the possibilities, the breadth and depth of a human being; your soul is so much bigger than you think it is. 'I've come so that you might have life in all its fullness.' In the light of that statement what do we choose? Are we getting away from it, or are we getting into it?

It's all very romantic having a shed in the garden, but the Vaseline focus of it all scratches completely when it's minus four outside and the radiator simply can't compete. India was watching the holiday programme and there was Nice and the Promenade des Anglais, the casinos, the cars, the beaches, the markets, the endless blue at the end of the sea. We are struggling, we're up that creek financially. Both Jacs and I have temperatures. No wonder it all looks so appealing. It snowed today, huge chunks of bleached candyfloss. Hopefully the frost will freeze it tight.

I was asked to preach at Ely Cathedral this morning. This is a once-a-year outing for the Kings School. It must be hell for them on a Monday morning: stand up, sit down, sing, sit down again, stand up again. I was trying to persuade them that Valentine's Day is very important: it was the first time, the first delicate trial of their own understanding of love, it was now their turn to do it their way. Our true love given freely is the greatest gift we can ever give to another human being.

You have to get involved as a priest – it's an essential part of what you do. How many times have you heard, 'You have to remain detached' from psychotherapists and the medical profession or 'The secret is not to get involved'? It doesn't work being a vicar – the exact opposite is what it's all about. Some priests save themselves or spare themselves; they end up by switching off; all that remains is your recording of stock phrases. I have some; they come out sometimes and when they do I am not listening, not recognising, not feeling, because I'm tired, annoyed, whatever. I did hear of one priest who got to the point where he could not see the family before a funeral. He would arrange it all on the phone, then turn up and press the same old buttons. The undertakers who told me this said they knew the service off by heart. Breathing that chloroform is far too easy. It simply involves closing down to other people and to God. God can be very difficult because the unspoken language, the knowing of God which seems totally complete, the way in which God knows you is not always easy to acknowledge. When we reduce that to what God was when we dared to listen or to what the books say, then we are as good as dead. There is, as far as I can see, no personal gain in opening yourself up to others, in being vulnerable, in being alive to every letter of every word for its own sake. But there are times, and they cannot be conjured up, when you lose all sense of self and are overwhelmed by a sense of complete love and a peace that passes all understanding, when you are released from your own understanding and held in something far more simple.

The Worship Group was more of a group therapy session really; we sat in Tony's sitting room, safe behind the walls of a self-imposed womb. We agreed that what was said would go no further. Next month we have the job of trying to link the back and the front of the church umbilically.

The bishop talked yesterday about the motion passed on homosexuality at Lambeth. He said the lobbying on both sides had hardened the debate; handfuls of fliers passed out, forcing each side's cause. The room was packed full of vicars. They say that all professions en masse are pretty awful; we seem to conveniently forget that when it comes to the House of Commons. But we are drab, there's no other word for it. We seem to have the complexion of digestive biscuits, we drink halves, we all look like we've just taken off duffel coats, we look tired, awkward under neon.

The service station on the M4 was a place between science fiction and a fun fair. There was not one point of silence; hard faces, hard lips swelling on cigarettes, caught in a constant storm of computer car engines, gunfire on the killing game, a pound a go. The fruit machines piped their jingles, the lights on the panels were programmed for repeating orgasms. The shop had rows of dream titles, dream cars, dream boats, surfboards, fishermen, yachts, steam engines, art, music, sex everywhere, sweets the colour of chemicals, flesh pulled under perspex, banks of sandwiches. As you went through the door a young man was there to greet you, the Bank of Connecticut was willing to take your debt in less than two minutes. There were burgers, scones, tandoori chicken, nine types of mineral water, twenty different soft drinks, the tables were set in lines, close crammed. There were posters placed above each urinal; the official spokesman for car crime had a leather face, shaved head, eyes that had seen fists: 'one car is stolen every thirty seconds'. There is no escape, you walk in and you become a captive. You're there to eat, to buy, you can't even piss for free. The view has been bought. I always resented the fact that at school – I went to a cold and brutal public school – the lower half of the windows had frosted glass in all the upper-storey classrooms. I remember once standing on the windowsill to look out – it was the first day the clocks went back, the sky was fired orange. The distance was impenetrable in the overwhelming colour. This was a forbidden sight – perhaps that made it more vivid.

It's Sunday tomorrow. Sarah is back, I saw her briefly at

Henry's funeral. She always makes me feel better – she makes everyone feel better. Maybe we should rent her out to stand at the automatic doors of service stations, to shake your hand. Imagine if they were places of rest. That is what they should be; at the moment they are no more than retail war zones, you're a target the moment you get out of the car.

The Archbishop of Canterbury is said to be emotionally and physically exhausted. Eight years is a long time, and it looks to have been a rough ride. The turmoil of the last thirty years has left a very tired infrastructure. The pressures to simply keep everything going within a group of parishes is immense, and there are far too many exhausted priests. As an institution we desperately need change – not for its own sake, but to try to create a system that isn't at breaking point all the time. The buzz word at the moment is that the church is a 'voluntary organisation'; that's true, but it's not an excuse for the shambolic way it's managed. We are also not the only voluntary organisation: there are thousands of them that manage not to leave their employees perpetually strung out. With forty-one dioceses there is too much duplication of work. The system of largely independent clergy looks very good on paper but their workload is immense. The problem with the multi-parish system is that you're in a no-win situation – you simply cannot satisfy every single demand made upon you. Creative change, crumbling buildings, fundraising, simply get left out in what should be a pastorally centred ministry.

The main problem is the open secret that the way things are now, in terms of structure of the organisation, cannot continue. It is totally unacceptable for the church, the ministry, to burn people out, to leave them disorientated and exhausted, martyrdom at the expense of keeping the show on the road. To be fair, no one ever said it was going to be easy, but impossible demands have three consequences. Nothing gets done properly – which is the most common visible manifestation of where we are at the moment. The second possibility is people simply get fed up with it all and leave, or plod on with their heads down talking about retirement for twenty years. The third is that there is an increasing acceptance of personal failure, as you are implicated in one public-relations disaster after another and are unable to achieve anything that is demanded of you.

The church has always been desperately arrogant: we are sure we have God with us and that God would not consort with journalists, graphic designers, quantity surveyors and management consultants; we have contented ourselves with talking shop, reassured our egos by performing theological twists and turns and perhaps become so engrossed in our own ideas that we fail to notice that no one is buying anything any more. We have buildings but no builders, walls but no painters, words but no writers. The lines we drew in the sand with our ringed fingers were trodden on long ago; they do not exist any more, they do not exist in people's imaginations. Capitalism walked over them without a word. Far from raging about a society sick with greed, we believe our survival depends in large part on the spoils of that dirty war. Jimmy McGovern's beautifully written drama 'The Lakes' has a character in it who goes to the Catholic priest, who happens to be having an affair with his girlfriend's mother. A failing priest, I'm sure, makes everyone feel much better about themselves. Anyway, this character says to the priest that all he offers is pain. He questions whether this is the right prescription to deal with evil. What he is saying, perhaps, is that the result of sin is pain. There can be no doubt about that; he blamed the priest essentially for defining sin and thus imposing this pain on everyone else, that far from offering bliss there was also agony in his basket: 'You have given us ghosts in your silent way, led us into walls. Find the door, you say.' Perhaps we will lose the right to impose our morality, to be judge and jury, especially if it's looking so user-unfriendly, so inconvenient. We've been sitting at the rich man's table for too long. Maybe the ultimate legacy of tolerance is a truly guilt-free existence, but Baal is sure to turn up sooner or later under the banner of free choice. We never really bargained for choice, it's not something we've ever had to deal with, but at least the signs are that we're beginning to wrestle with it now.

March . . . .

The woodpigeons have started singing again, the flushed notes which sit so comfortably with the trees rise in the morning now. They are not flying yet, the clapping wings forming a crescendo and then the slow release as they gently glide down. Haslingfield was barren this morning. It's half-term; there were only twenty-six of us. It looked lost. Sarah did her best to smile alone, which made up the spaces. The light hitting the pillars was the main feature. Anne preached. She took us into the wilderness; I wish she had left us there. The new baptism service is awful, there is no delight in it. It's heavy, it's been written with a heavy hand, it's been through a very rigid committee and has come out the other side as processed religion. I am amazed that people still want their children baptised – it's wonderful that they do; the promises they make on behalf of the child are probably the ones that are broken most often. As a society we push a lot of steam when marriage vows are broken, but no fuss is made about baptism vows; in purely religious terms they are far more serious than the marriage vows. The church either needs to operate some very tight boundaries here or the service needs to be made more realistic, certainly more accessible. It's Oxford this evening.

The service at Exeter College, Oxford, was dripping with
Catholic wine; it was packed full of these sweet faces that sang
seriously and matched the mosaics behind the altar. I was
never one of them. I had none of their sense, they were so
bright, so sure. Imagine being treated like that, imagine having
what you thought valued at that age; hopefully they will value
others in the same way. I ranted really, scolded, that we were
being pickled in history and that the trend of preservation
meant that the relationship between God and humanity was
showing fatigue. Conventional wisdom says when a marriage
runs out of petrol, this is sublimated in a frenzy of decorating.
Carpets aren't things you make love on any more; well, only
if you're completely sure they match the curtains first. Handy
Andy has probably intervened in more marriages than the
church, but there we go. It was hypocritical; here we are
spending half a million pounds on the tower. Imagine if that
money was used to create something. The main problem is if
you see everything as finished. Exeter College Chapel looks
so complete – we are left to polish and protect, to maintain;
we are not expected to create. We have been given something
that is apparently finished. We have become curators of faith,
guardians of liturgy, fixing on tradition. This generation will
have repainted a few bricks and replaced a few panes of glass.
The argument as to whether the buildings and the liturgy are
suitable for the current generation will largely have vaporised
in this obsession with the past.

If the Easter campaign has shown one thing, it is that a
religion based on the cultural niceties of a past age very soon
becomes history. It may feel safe back there, safe from the
onslaught of punk, pulp fiction and Happy Meals. Why is it that

the fresh and immediate, living and breathing creative force of God is presented as if we are struggling to escape the cramps of rigor mortis? We have turned the lamb of God into mutton. The cup of Christ is not to preserve us but to enlighten us. Maybe it is because we cannot bear the thought of our own death, our own impermanence, that we allow ourselves to believe in the mirage of permanence; we cannot face anything transitory. We love the rhythm of the returning swallows but we have misinterpreted the permanence of God and attached ourselves to it in the vain hope that eternity will rub off on our red cheeks somehow. The funeral service is beautiful in this respect: dust to dust, ashes to ashes, earth to earth. We can only ever take part in a cycle, ride the storm; we are travellers, all of us, travellers in time, as indeed Christ was. We can sing in Latin if we want, we can read Hebrew, chew Greek, trawl the inside of words for meaning we cannot be completely sure of, but the disciples, Mary Magdalene, however, were the same as us. As human as we are, they might not look human, really human, etched in black lines in the Bible, but that's what they were. What happened is all the more incredible; because of that we have put them out of reach. To presume they had an unblemished silver line to God is legendary nonsense. A just God would not favour one generation over another. To give them a golden age simply denies it to our own. They would surely not want us to dote on them either, no; these illusions of permanence were thriving in the Jewish temple in Jerusalem at the time of Christ. No wonder Christ scared the living daylights out of all of them; our flesh has no right to be eternal. Maybe this desire for permanence and the illusion of it is why we treat this planet so appallingly. If it is made by God it cannot possibly let us down, we can simply go on taking and taking from the land, from the sea, felling and forcing. Perhaps it is as permanent as we are; this inspired religious illusion will cost us dear. Travellers, nomads, do not over-graze because they understand they will need the pasture again. Modern farming can best be described as hit and run, smash and grab. The notion that businesses can own genes is nothing other than corporate theft, their manipulation of this material to their own ends also demonstrates how unfit they are to be guardians of it.

There are some new books called pocket canons. What is so fine about them is that they are blatantly fashionable. The Gospel of John has a black and white cover, people streaming up the side of a hill; Song of Solomon has a woman with bee-stung lips. The words are not styled looking like tombstones; most Bibles still have that feel: *Holy Bible* written in a granite face, awful. Parish noticeboards generally look like they are welcoming you to H.M. Prison Parkhurst, with a list of visiting times underneath, painful, the folly of permanence again. Pub signs actually offer far more *joie de vivre* than we do. No, these new books will look old in ten years' time and we'll have to design some more. I must read what Will Self has to say about Revelation; now there's a sojourner.

It's all over for churchmanship. I was reliably informed this morning that the new all-inclusive word for describing your own particular bent was church style. So we're not allowed to ask people about their churchmanship any more, the new question is 'What style are you?', 'What church style do you practice?' It's a great word, style, a manipulation of thread for effect: barbed-wire hats, flannel and fleece, feathers for trousers. Imagine choir robes designed by Vivienne Westwood – I think she should – pews by Richard Rogers, windows by

Rodney Fitch, all lit by the late Derek Jarman.

The Bishop of Ely tells this story. At the end of the Second World War a parish priest was promised a field full of strawberries. The church put out the news to the whole village, who assembled in the village hall to eat their fill. The cream which the church had organised did not materialise, and neither did the strawberries. The parish priest had the unfortunate task of announcing this, but he said that instead of the strawberries and cream the church had gone to great lengths and organised prunes and custard. This was greeted by a plural groan. The bishop goes on to say that much of the church is prunes and custard. The image is absolutely right, the sense it conjures up is perfect; while it may reflect the church, it is a million miles from the God we struggle to represent. It will not and cannot sustain us.

Wedding rehearsals are always strange events. These people arrive in ordinary clothes and we bang on about the bones of the service. They hand over a brown envelope full of cash and that's about the sum of it. They usually spend longer milling around afterwards, talking flowers and aunts. Tomorrow they will say the words for themselves. We've had little success translating God beyond the words we use. Maybe that is the purpose of bricks and paint; I hope so.

Josh has been around now for two and half weeks. Jacs and I have been giving him breakfast and sometimes supper. He's sleeping in the bus shelter by the post office. He's twenty-four years old; unless people feed him, he would starve. It's impossible to see his face, he's done up in layers of shirts and coats. The fear he generates is spectacular: mothers hold their children tight, very few people look him in the eye. This is leprosy really, hardly surprising he has befriended the bottle.

He drank four of them yesterday, sparkling cider, 99 p a hit. It was the first time I'd seen him smile, this face of a child in a beaming stupor. Fear spawns the best lies; they're always so plausible, so reasonable, so well conceived, comfortable lies. They start small, nothing too demanding, nothing so terrible: you take pencils which don't belong to you, just little things. Once you start lying, to justify, to protect whatever honourable reason it is, you are out of your depth, your soul is under water. There are some awful islands out there, we all know what they are. Josh is on Alcohol Island.

I'm fed up with working, it's all I've done. Eat, sleep, work. There are all these Lent meetings on Wednesday nights, so I guess I've given up football. The phone never stops, the doorbell goes on and on, the bank are on our backs, somewhere there is a clock without time, some sand without feet, the little terns will be nesting up on Scolt Head Island soon; I must go and sleep there again. I'm on Job's Island right now.

One of the main illusions about walking in the mountains is that you believe you're free of the valleys, the towns, the bells on the shop doors, televisions slung in the corners of dark pubs, the leaves blown along roads. Scaféll is an extraordinary lump of rock. If you walk up from Cockley Beck up the path, then dip down over the water, follow the sheep, follow the steep-falling stream to the ridge then up to the summit. Maybe the therapy of screaming lungs and rotting legs just adds to the isolation of the top.

Jimmy McGovern writes in his own blood perhaps. His portrayal of the Catholic church has all the hallmarks of a vendetta: the hapless priest sleeping with someone else's wife; the bishop justifying abortion to keep the church clean, so we can all hope that the illusion is not tattered, the cellophane that separates church and people is not torn. The souls outside the sacred walls can take coke, have affairs and kill each other, that's all right; they've opted for a Godless heaven. There seems to be little sympathy for priests who break their vows. There's usually a sense of relief on one hand – we are as human as everyone else – and disappointment on the other that we are as human as everyone else. If you want us to hold the line, if you would like to measure your own success against our failings, go ahead; it's a mug's game though. There are going to be priests that fail to live up to the demands of their job. I am definitely one of them, along with all the rest. Catholic, Protestant, Methodist, Orthodox, they're all the same, mate, we can't hack it, there's only been one human being that managed it ever. Yes, I'm a hypocrite, a liar and a two-faced bastard, what on earth makes you think I'm any different from you? If you want beauty, truth, grace and love then start praying. Don't take the mickey out of us because we can't live up to it either; no one ever said we would or we could. The pages of the New Testament are riddled with failure, thank God. Maybe we are stupid enough to keep failing, but as long as we are failing we are also trying. It's not like a ring pull, a packet of biscuits: there are no equations, no sounds, there are no cooking instructions, someone somewhere had to jump out of the plane and try the first parachute. Most priests do that every day and as most people know they don't always open.

Tippex is no more, he was stiff and cold, his head buried in the sawdust. We buried him in the garden. He has finally escaped.

We have four mice. We did have three mice – one was left alone in the shop. But I'm afraid I fell for the 'You cruel and heartless man' line and charged back into Cambridge and rescued the remaining mouse. They are quite beautiful – piebald, black and white. India's is brown, brown and white.

Small Boat, Big Sea

They shiver with life.

I was coming back from the Queen's Head last night and stopped the car just over the bridge from Harlton. The cool air coming in between the leafless trees felt new, as if it had just been unpacked. Our skin hardens, perhaps, as we age, as it fails to renew itself so often; we're left holding onto the old stuff for much longer. There's a scene in *Women in Love* where Oliver Reed and Alan Bates sit down naked in some long grass that's wet with dew or rain; they played it as fascinated animals, enchanted by the overwhelming sense of it all. Our worship, although sensory, is not madly sensual; we worship so much with words it's all very one-dimensional. They are jammed into lines laid out in an 'O'-level style. Think how much more invigorating baptism would be if we threw a bucket of water over the candidate. I caught the tail end of a talk on healing the other night; she was saying how important touch was, the laying on of hands, our awareness of healing involved in touch, our own potential to heal, our need to be healed. The climax of the ordination service is this laying on of hands. I remember being made a priest; it broke me completely. Maybe we have formalised something that Christ did naturally. Our need for understanding and order has left us feeble when it comes to taking risks. Even worse is when you feel an overwhelming temptation to ask permission beforehand. Priests probably go one of two ways: they're either drawn into the establishment or they draw away from it. I'm always deeply suspicious of why any priest should want more than they already have. Surely right now the moment is more than enough, rich beyond our dreaming. Ambition involves complicity in the act of self-serving, and self-service compromises most of us in the end – pollutes.

I've asked Sarah to choose the people to do the laying on of hands. We're going to have a service on the third Sunday in April; instead of communion we'll have healing, touch instead of taste. I drove Josh back to his village this afternoon; I hope he's at home, it's all wind and rain outside. It all ended in dilemma. Experienced voices saying, don't feed him, it's simply not helping him and Christian conscience saying, give him caviar and champagne, an electric blanket and endless love. I accept in conventional terms that the food wasn't what he needed. He did the most incredible things to this village: on one hand he caused terminal tension and on the other he spawned genuine charity and concern. He disturbed us beautifully. He asked some very difficult questions, the main one being how Christian is Christian, he litmus-tested all of us. The most wonderful thing is I have no idea whether we passed or failed; only he knows that.

On Wednesday mornings in Haslingfield we have a short communion service. It's not threatened with change, there's laughter and intimacy. It's something to really look forward to. The Sunday services have a different feel; it's all beginning to calm down a bit now, the tension is relaxing slowly. From a management perspective a first-time priest might provide the tonic to change things, but change isn't always needed. Everyone sees the priest as the kindly figure but the job can be brutal at times. You may live up to some people's expectations but for others you are a nightmare, you are the antithesis of what they feel a priest should do and say. I know I'm letting people down, I'm not the priest they want, I'm not the priest actually that they need. Surely the whole idea of the body of Christ is that we love each other equally and without favour. Natural affinity wreaks havoc: your face, your shoes, your hands, your breath, your voice, these are surely not things to be overcome, but we all reek of them. In the age of the individual they shine more than they should, perhaps. You have to hang on to love. Fashion is essentially about being judged on labels not thread; we are completely overcome once they define us. If you are content to be defined by your laces, by your house, by your car, by your holiday, then you have fallen for the oldest trick in the book: what happens when we all have street cred? Where do we go from there? Designer wars, coming to a street near you?

The young people of East London University were all eyes. Communication and religion was their module. About fifty of them were there to hear about the Easter campaign. They asked fantastic questions. 'In the age of the image does it matter what colour Christ was?' 'How long would the revolutionary image we have produced last?' 'Was Jesus middle-class?' 'Is there a true image of Christ?' Imagine if there was. Perhaps the most wonderful thing is that there is not. We're not left with any photographs of Jesus caught bored, no yawning, no bouncing footage of the sermon on the mount, no tourist camera to catch him walking on water. So what we have, all of it, is invention, except for the tantalising Turin Shroud, perhaps. To be attached to any of it is to have fallen for Catholic style, for solid Evangelical colours; all he has left you with are some translated words and your imagination: one thin thread, that's all. From it we have made an endless tapestry; you may not like it, but the fact, which history bears out, that anything has been made at all is nothing short of incredible. The fact that each generation has come along and added to it, burnt some of it, trodden on it, is almost incidental. In that sense no image is holy; the icon only serves the artist because it's supposition.

I can't decide whether the Sistine Chapel is worship or art. If it is worship then it challenges our paltry lack of anything contemporary to live up to it. If it is art then it is supposition, one man's journey to his own limits. But still, in the absence of any video footage, it all becomes art history. The problem is we are reading it rather than making it; worse still, preserving it, creating the end of it all, a time when we actually stopped imagining for ourselves.

The pope is coming in for a lot of flak for agreeing to have his voice treated in a studio for being dubbed into rap, the CD hasn't arrived yet but it's on its way. There are the usual calls of, 'This is devaluing Christianity', 'We should be concentrating on the issues of poverty, justice, love and grace.' He is. Rap, the music of anger and arrogance, pomp and posture, is the champion of a self-proclaimed under-class who feel deeply ignored and mistreated. Firstly, the critics of his action have missed that one completely, and secondly, this isn't a disagreement over the message. The critics are far more concerned with the medium, that God is singing to the rhythm of a road drill. This is about a culture, not a consciousness. This is about preserving God, not proclaiming God. The world must be redeemed from rap, from rave, from Damien Hirst. Will Self's introduction to Revelation is fascinating, after all he's human clay, there is a world in that ink, the world where I find God because of itself, a God not encased in the paraphernalia of the church.

To separate Saturday nights from Sunday mornings, have we not placed God in our own custody? Is a coach full of earnest Christians going on a retreat more holy than a bus full of Luton Town supporters? We say they must recognise God, see Christ as the saviour of their souls. They must all be saved, saved from themselves, saved from the dance floor, saved from Silverstone, saved from sex. But you can't take a funeral without accepting that perfection is an elixir we only sip at. To say that struggling is limited to those who struggle to reconcile the eternal words of Christ to their own lives is nonsense. All human life involves struggle, this journey is not an easy one for any of us. Belief in God does not make it easier – if anything it actually becomes harder, because you have to accept sin, your own part in it – how it defaces others, is anti-life. You bring on yourself judgment upon judgment. Yes, reconciliation with the father of your soul will also reveal your own unbearable beauty. Sin is perhaps far more bearable because it denies true beauty, and hideous truth. You don't have to deal with it, you can simply fall asleep, become unconscious to the corridors of your soul.

Have we not taken God out of the world and put him, put her, into church, for our own practical convenience, done up Sundays in buttons. There is a row going on over an Alleluia Service which took place in the cathedral last Sunday, emails flying out that it is wrong to say Alleluia in Lent; this is probably from the same computers biting that flowers are an outrage too. This is about law not love, content not consciousness. It's so strange that – while the grass ferments in a warm yeast, the elderberry blossom chimes, the primroses seep between large green leaves, the purple altarcloth is there in every violet – the churches should be bare, and even worse that it should be important. It's Wednesday March 10th, it's dour with clouds, the sunlight comes in shocking seconds, the birds have started dancing now. Alleluia.

The church clock has been tampered with. The time difference is becoming more extreme – it has leapt forward thirteen minutes since Sunday. Is this a mysterious hand to get me to start on time?

It was Mothering Sunday today. It was everything English, the Brownies in the front row, an essential mix of old and young. The old church looked quite full in Haslingfield. I always enjoy it when we start the service with a silence. I stand there and pompously say 'Let's just have a few moments silence, wait upon the presence of God.' This morning God was laughing, giggling loudly at the back. Layla had disturbed our calm earlier on in the week; she had been to a service in Oakington. The vicar there has the Holy Spirit running after him and is a benchmark for all that is good within the church. Layla came back and told me that while she was speaking in tongues she had a very clear sense that God was saying, 'They know about me, but they don't know me.' That short sentence was directed at the churches here. What precision, that one breath should contain both our failings and our possibilities. Today we went through the motions again, we handed out flowers, we sang, we sat.

Boy George last night was running over the New Romantics Top Ten, boys in blusher, Adam Ant talking to the floor, Sheffield in chiffon. They went for it, didn't they? They took it to the wire, cut it and walked through. You don't have to like it, intellectually it didn't draw the same red punk blood. What we forget is that Christianity was a youth movement: it had the same hit, it was daring and extreme and definitely offensive in parts. We're not going to overcome greed by being reasonable and accommodating – the last hundred years bears that out. Maybe it's a craving for sanity, the fact that so much of what you see of the church is sensible.

Yes, we walk on water, some of us heal, we talk with God; it's all ludicrous, all of it. To compensate we go to extraordinary lengths to please, to flatter, to reassure that this is all normal and acceptable and most of all unthreatening; hence perhaps the ruddy great chasm between knowing and knowing about;

it is a reaction. The best thing I can think of about doing this job is that you are right there at the sharp end, that it hurts, that in terms of the rational you are left with snowflakes in your hand, looking at the patterns in the falling leaves. They are there if you want to look.

As a priest I've really had to give up living by the materialist yardstick – it hasn't been easy. From that perspective a Lamborghini is no more than a toy, wealth becomes fantastically unimportant, you are out of the loop. The liberation is intense, your life spins around phrases like becoming poor to become rich which appear at first as a riddle, but they begin to make sense. Your internal life becomes external, it is a simple matter really of placing your soul before your body, your heart before your mind. The changes although subtle are real. In a secular sense, for instance, body always precedes soul: your body and soul, feed the body to feed the soul. The religious expression is the other way round: soul and body. We're always told there is a massive gulf between the two but, raving religious or ardent atheist, we still are working with the same material, we just see and sense it differently, that's all. They're not actually poles apart at all. Walking on water isn't just a matter of faith; it's actually a matter of physics as well. To divide the act with science and religion does justice to neither of them. There is real pain as well: you have to bear pain, and other people's pain. You are constantly reminded of death and in it your own. I'm sure everyone responds differently but for me dealing with death has hardened a sense of how completely fragile all of this is: you and I living on air. Sometimes I end up railing against God for the total injustice of it all, but most of all life is made more precious because it appears to be so fragile. It is laced with wonder, every second. Some vicar is saying give us the money instead: he didn't want a vicarage, he wanted a mortgage. No, I want a vicarage. I think it's a very good system not owning things. We should perhaps earn less not more. The first Brimstones were flying today; it was warm, there were two of them out by the old wall, yellow dots dancing on the film, racing for food and sex before the frost returns.

The posters went up today in glamorous Kenington Road. There was a small battalion of cameras, all aimed at the Bishop of Southwark standing on a wobbly ladder holding what looked like a tickling stick; it was the glue brush. The site looked good. We're using the four-sheet posters to make up the forty-eight sheets, which gives the whole thing a Sandinista style that works well with the message of revolution. A friend called me earlier to say that Ann Widdecombe was playing the part of outraged Conservative MP again. The poster also made an appearance in the *Face* under the sub 'Resurrection Man'. The copy ended by saying that the *Daily Mail* had asked for those responsible for it to be excommunicated, which, as far as the *Face* is concerned, gave the whole thing a massive boost of credibility, not that it really needs one. It has apparently been the most successful Easter campaign we've ever produced.

I've been coughing up blood, in rich red spoonfuls. I've got to go for an X-ray; the doctor wouldn't make light of it which is just as well as the pains in my chest are persistent at least. My imagination is charging with the possibilities of death. I lost a friend last year to cancer – we were the same age. Today it's a release really, life is not a sentence necessarily. We are surely here to learn to love, learn to love ourselves. It's not about sinking or swimming – these are hard and human judgments – it is about walking on water. You see, why did he do it? There was no need. Yes, you could say it was to demonstrate divinity, but there are all the other miracles. I do believe he did it – I don't want to know how, but we are surely asked all of us to follow him, to the cross, to the temple, into the wilderness, to the wedding, to the mountains and, yes, across the water.

I was summoned by the back of the church on Saturday afternoon. What direction was the church going in, how were we going to get there, what vision did I have? We talked for a couple of hours but there was nothing I could say other than I felt that in the midst of so many competing views I spent too much time holding it all together. This perhaps is what bishops do on a grander scale. The Bishop of Ely said that trying to inspire clergy with a sense of vision was akin to herding cats. I took the posters round all the city-centre churches yesterday and came away feeling very sorry for myself. It was remarks like 'Oh, we're in between curates here and yes, this year we're stacked out with weddings, we have three of them'; 'Last year was unusual as well, we had two funerals.' It was the office staff that informed me of these bare facts. The brutal fact is that rural ministry is failing, it cannot compete, it is under-resourced, under-manned and undermined. The multi-parish thing has to go, or the expectations that go with it have to change or be changed, or I have to change or be changed; it is exhausting. I have four churches to maintain as opposed to one. At the PCC meeting in Haslingfield last night, I just about gave up. We've canned the idea of building in the church, we've gone for some parish rooms on a small piece of glebe land. That seems the most sensible option in the face of a burgeoning Sunday school. After two years' worth of discussion we've decided that all the loos should be there. But there were no plans, because no one had made any, nothing was presented because no one had the time to do it, so muggins here looked completely outflanked.

That doesn't bother me really; what really started boiling

blood was this turned to complaint that nothing had happened, that industry would never work this way, could never work this way, that it was a shambles. Maybe this is all down to management prowess but if people say they are going to take responsibility for things and then don't, covering the fact up by devolving responsibility to the rest of us, the whole plan starts wavering. Maybe I should have chased them up, maybe that's the job I should have done before. But it's no good giving responsibility out only to have it bounce back at you all the time.

But that is my problem, not theirs. I'm not convinced we can do this; ultimately, people might not actually have the time. It's a full-time job. The man who does it here does it very thoroughly, neatly prepared reports, 'T's crossed 'I's dotted, but he's retired and really he does it as a full-time job, fills in all the forms, talks to the architects, organises the faculties and grants. There would have been no money to rebuild the tower without him: he's done an amazing job. Maybe it's the job of those people in the parish offices I saw in the city, sitting at organised desks at ease, relaxed; the hard fact is I'm not sure we could ever afford it. Perhaps we are looking at Haslingfield becoming the centre and Harlton and the Eversdens satellites – maybe that's the future – but multi-parish rural benefices are by and large failing because the job of management is frankly impossible. There needs to be much more work done at theological colleges on rural ministry other than an hour or two talking about farmers.

It's Palm Sunday. Both the four-sheet posters I've put up have been mysteriously knocked out by the wind; more worrying is the fact that there isn't any wind at all. For ten fleeting seconds I let myself believe that they had been nicked and this was a sure sign of their value. The truth was actually that they were crumpled and scratched down in the drain. Tom sent me a note he'd written to the bishop. As a result of our efforts, a member of the archbishops' council wants to join the team; whether this is with a watching brief or a creative brief has yet to be revealed.

The service this evening was the best service we've ever had in Haslingfield – there was a real sense of God. I've come to trust this sense. In it you lose your sense of time and almost place. When Paul speaks of being 'taken up' he is right; you definitely become part of the presence, you become intimately involved with it, it is both a forgetting and a revealing, you are released from your sense of self – it is an unknowing. Your body becomes unnecessary, every single cell is stilled. This is not a dumbing or the dull padding of opium. It is being held, not held in submission. It is being held in the way that you would hold something that was incredibly fragile, that you marvelled at. Does God marvel at his own, at her own creation? I'm sure this sense of wonder – the wonder we experience – is part of the paint of the image we are all made in.

The chest X-ray, the CAT scan, the blood tests, the breathing test, all seemed to be fine. My lungs are scarred from smoking, which apparently is not good for my age; they don't recover, apparently. If I stop now they won't scar any more. So stop I must, two days on Scolt Head should do it, off with the terns and oyster catchers. Death and I took a long hard look at each other last week. It's easy to be poetic about it, pulling on a roll-up and drinking gorgeous Adnams, but it was a bad trip. I was off with the Jabberwocky. God was there, fat hand on the lottery button. As a priest you deal with death all the time but perhaps I had just been dealing with it. You learn very quickly that this is a random percentages game, that your chance of dying goes up with each passing year, that there is no rhyme, no reason, as to who dies when or why, that continuing to breathe is just about staying ahead of the odds. Yes indeed, our days are but as grass. It was my response to it, my own death, that was so riddled with failure. I read about this bishop once who having been diagnosed accepted it completely, didn't fight it, didn't flinch, didn't hate it, didn't feel cheated by it, frightened by it, he just went with it; there was no gasping for air, no drugs. I was leaving Las Vegas, writing torn notes, screaming at God in the mire of it all. But it was my own mire – I had created it. Given an infinite number of directions I could have taken, that's where I went.

We read the passage from Mark today about Peter denying he knew Christ. You think, how could he have done that? You judge, you point fingers, wallow in *Schadenfreude*. It's not a ridiculous story though, not in the context. It's about being frightened and isolated, it's about running up drainpipes. I ran.

Liebskinder, Liebskinder, what wild buildings, wall upon wall, light cracking, bricks split, jungles of angles sliced into spaces, yes! They had no dust yet, no warm stones, but so what – the moss will only do them good. These buildings, his buildings, are inspired by the clouds. Imagine if they were uniform: same shape, same size, cruising in on cue. No, they are free-formed as you are, they speak in semiotics, words without letters, songs without notes, pictures without paint. Tavener writes like that.

Kosovo is burning still, tractors trundling over the borders crammed with defeated faces. They seem to sit there in silence; maybe there is nothing to say at the moment. It must raise a dreadful ghost to know that another human like yourself can kill so easily. This is about the future, a principle, and the

Serbs are caught on the point; it is politics practised in a hall of mirrors, nobody actually knows what's going on and why. Even the propaganda looks confused. At best you could say this is a new world order where human rights become the new lexicon of martyrdom. They are dying for God – it's an old-fashioned thing. We don't die for God any more, we die so that you can be free on our terms. The reward for your suffering will be a fast track to the websites of the West, where at the touch of a button everything there can be yours.

I'm not convinced any more that national parks are a good idea. Their existence forces us to feel better about our dreadful treatment of the environment. We can all jump in the car and visit them, these apparent safe zones, the dry stone walls, ravens and sheep. But the very fact that they are exclusive means that it's open season for everything around them. Conservation is a nonsense, if it is only allowed in certain areas. If Wimpy and McAlpine are not allowed to build their dull and predictable ghettos within the boundaries of the national park, why are they permitted to build them elsewhere? It's the same rain that falls on the heather and pavements alike. But it's treated very differently once it dries.

We had compline tonight. Sarah and I moved a few things around today, just a bookstand and a noticeboard; it made a huge difference. There are services every night this week and on Friday we're carrying a cross from Great Eversden to Haslingfield. I had lunch with two journalists from *Time* magazine who wanted to know why the English parish priest was so eternally fascinating, so eccentric. We sat in the Queen's Head; there was a party of pilgrims carrying a cross to Walsingham outside. Innocent features: they were out of place, their faces would have been better suited to the trailers coming in from Kosovo. It's a ludicrous thing to do, to walk all that way. As a piece of PR it is in part a self-fulfilling parody, but perhaps that is the way it is seen. To take part in it, I'm sure, feels very different indeed.

April

It's Good Friday. There is a spiteful sky, brooding. Yesterday was a blazing blue, the butterflies were out dreaming. There still haven't been any Orange Tips – maybe they'll venture out after Easter. We spent last night packing, Jacs and the children are going to Norfolk today. We've rented a cottage for a week. The rent was paid for by the Friends of the Clergy who sent a very large cheque which also included the fees for play school, which was very generous indeed. I thought it might dent the overdraft, which at the moment is about four and a half grand, but there was another letter from the bank this morning telling us that we have once again slipped over the limit. It's a constant struggle. After Easter Sunday vicars are allowed what's called the inside of a week off. You have to go away to get it. You really have to leave the parishes to have any time off at all – the phone and the doorbell don't stop ringing just because it happens to be your day off or you happen to be on holiday. I picked up twenty hot cross buns this morning, six quid. We'll start with those before our walk. We'll carry the heavy cross from Great Eversden to Haslingfield, about three miles; a photographer should be appearing from the local paper at some point.

◆ ◆ ◆

The plum tree is in blossom, bee-wing petals tied in tight bundles, fit for a bride. I still haven't passed the pruning test. It's all very haphazard watching for the blossom, watching the bark, wondering what's coming. Jacs is away with the children; the house is alive with their ghosts, their fingerprints are everywhere. I'm going to shoot off to Norfolk after the service at Harlton tomorrow. It took us about two days to pack. Sarah came round with some chocolate bunnies, an African violet and a bottle of Jacob's Creek, so I'll ferry them up tomorrow. There is a real stillness now; the fields have a layer of mist all over them, the sap is rising, spring is rushing in, everything caught in adolescence. A friend sent me some shots he had taken of an ex-girlfriend of mine. His timing was perfect. Was it Oscar Wilde that said youth is wasted on the young? I disagree, it is wasted on the old: the young are the only ones wise enough to waste it. It was lovely to see her like that, naked again; we left each other in that same state.

The walk carrying the cross was, as always, interesting – to see the faces of those rushing by in their cars; they never quite look you in the eye. We chatted all the way to Harlton and then walked in silence on to Haslingfield. There were all ages, pushchairs and walking sticks. We all took it in turns to carry the cross; it is heavy, about sixty to seventy pounds. Today is Easter Saturday, it is ripe with patience. The patience of God is immeasurable; this notion of punishment, of God killing, spitting on us has cankered roots. It's the cane all over again: behave or I will hurt you. This is not the God I know. The desolation we experience is when we abandon God – God does not abandon us. God did not put Christ on the cross, we did. We can fool ourselves if we like, we can make wars holy, we can insist that God is homophobic, we claim the authority of scripture, apostolic succession, but it's all expedient; the cause takes over from the causeway. Those ten days when death crept up close, I was crying and cursing, Why have you forsaken me, the good-time God, you know, the one that makes everything all right, Mr Happy Ending? He went down with the sun, I could not find him. God was there on the cross, at the lowest point of human history, the God of the gas chamber, the electric chair. Here God redeems the executed and the executioner. Why should he, why should she, favour either? The dark pathways we all crawl down, hiding from the moon, we are surely followed; it's perhaps whether we have the wherewithall at those points to take the hand that's always offered rather than biting it.

Easter Sunday started at 6.30 – we had a joint service with the chapel on Barrington Hill. There were about twenty-five of us in a circle. I was without the usual six o'clock start that Jonson and Harris normally provide. I must have slept through the alarm clock, so I arrived looking as though I had just got out of bed, which was the truth of it. Both churches were pretty full. A basket full of eggs came down from the bell chamber in Haslingfield to the charismatic children's arms below. Harlton was awash with flowers. The singing at Harlton is amazing – it can fill the place.

This is it: salt marshes, avocets, the sea breeze, Merlin's woods, North Norfolk and muddy waters. We're staying in a house in Cley. Freedom: the dog-collar's in the kennel. The boundary between the priest and the person is more relaxed now; they can coexist quite happily or they can come together without pressure. It's a wonderful job, but it makes too many martyrs, the parochialism is killing: cleaning the cobwebs, managing the money, mending the windows, making sure the grass is mown, sorting out the raffle, keeping the nettles down, all this becomes defining, it sticks in your throat. The North Sea is grey. I've rarely seen it blue, it's a leeward sea, wrestling with purgatory. This is the Church of England; there is always nothing exciting about it, is there? It's got Could Do Better stamped all over it, come on, love one another, make a scene about it; we have forgotten how to dance.

The sky on the sea was dragged off the Fens, the luminous edges outlining Constable colours. We sat on the beach, our hair crashing into our eyes, the wind tossing the kite into tangos. In the café on the beach which is dark inside, there are birds on the walls; the corrugated plastic rattles on the roof outside. We caught crabs this morning in Wells, pulling them up on orange lines out of the solemn water. The sun rushed through once in a while, turning the grey gulls white. We're just visiting, this is not our home, I'm sure of it; we are born pioneers and tourists. Watch the wildlife programmes – this is classic tourism, Planet Earth, a wonderland and a wasteland in perfect harmony. Did we choose to come here or have we been left to look for something?

We came back to two mice; we had left three, the fourth passed away some time ago. The third one had been just about consumed; feet, head, tail, all gone. This was a salutary lesson in the fact that what appeared to be sweet and fragile had acquired some very dangerous tastes. There is apparently a restaurant in the east where you can order a *Homo sapiens* fillet; there's a reluctant fascination in it, I should imagine. The chestnut trees have come out, the leaves seem exhausted – they lie without muscle, too soft to stand. The *Sunday Times* was on the phone yesterday; apparently the Bishop of Durham managed to burn a cool £160,000 on expenses and they wanted to make something of it. This was at least five vicars, so they told me – is a bishop worth five vicars? Should a bishop be measured in that way? I'm not unduly fussed about it. This wouldn't be shocking from a business perspective – for someone who works seven days a week and has a staff to pay it all seems pretty reasonable. Most of this I would imagine goes on maintenance; it is the cost of maintaining the office of bishop. Across the diocese this would probably come in at around three million pounds.

I think if we are spending that amount of money then we deserve more than rudderless and confused leadership – that is what it seems. But in reality bishops are there to perform pre-ordained tasks, they are part of a management model which is clearly way past its sell-by date, and a conservative culture that is self-perpetuating. The Crown Appointments Commission in that respect have been killing us. The evidence is all around you. We are also paying to maintain a structure which is based on privilege, a structure we cannot afford that was put in place centuries ago and is clearly incompatible with, and essentially at odds with, our contemporary culture. We use up more energy carrying it than anything else. If we are to survive we will need to become leaner and fitter. We will need to refocus completely, to become servants of a society that has rumbled the fact that we spend most of our energy serving ourselves. At the parish level the whole thing about expenses has become a bit of a nonsense really. Some parishes can afford to pay for all sorts of things: new cars, holidays, the odd shopping bill. The trouble is there's no parity; it's all down to whim, generosity and circumstance, where you happen to be. I've only been given money twice. Once when I was a curate someone handed me twenty quid after a funeral and the other day I was given nine pounds to buy a beer or two after the Mothers' Union service. That's it. Up in the Fens we had a couple of bags of spuds, and boxes of apples and pears used to appear periodically. There were wonderful strawberries too, but it's not like being a waiter at all. I think I earned more in tips as a petrol pump attendant. I remember as a child reading the polite pew notices on Easter Sunday which asked for generosity as the collection was going to the vicar. That doesn't happen any more, or if it does the amount is deducted from your stipend. I suppose it's an easier relationship; the parish share at least separates those who support the church financially from the vicar, albeit cosmetically. It makes sermons easier, if your income is not directly aligned to your popularity or the plague.

It's uneasy being back; you become aware of standing at the base of a mountain again. I'm increasingly concerned about the calendar, our focus on Easter and Christmas. We tend to indulge in triumphalism, the victory of Christianity. The victory of Christianity over what, over whom? None of this has much to do with actually living it. People just turn up for the party, God becomes locked in canned carols. We need to refocus. The Christian calendar has just become an excuse to head off to the coast. Quite rightly people have sussed it has nothing to do with God, that's surely the way it seems. It's also predictable, you know the punctuation, it's not working. These forms arrived from the diocese this morning asking us for the average attendance, how many people arrive at Easter and Christmas. Perhaps we should be less enthusiastic about Christmas; it might simply be reinforcing the problem. People turn up for the performance; maybe the puppet show should change.

The annual general meeting was less political this year. We always have it in the village hall which is new and dustless. Up on the Fens the village hall was an old chicken shed, all the light bulbs were coloured – greens, reds, blues, oranges. The whole place kept every echo, and when the lights were out the blue light from the garage next door would haunt the space inside. We used to have a youth club on Wednesday evenings and they would all pile in – that was a learning curve. Some of the ten-year-olds had the most silken football skills I'd ever seen. We'd eat chews and drink coke, I'd get thrashed at pool by some hot-shot seven-year-old and we'd just about reach nine o'clock with the hall still standing, having wiped the glass on the picture of the Parish Council clean again of some of the most extraordinary graffiti. It was the only picture in the vast room. I never found out who was doing it, or who stuck the French letter on the exhaust of my car. The hardest thing of all was keeping a straight face.

At the first hint of daylight Jonson is up immediately, tackling such thorny issues as how to untie a balloon from his bed. We've tried a six o'clock regime. There's a purple clock by his pillow, but his own internal alarm clock rings with the birds. It's quarter past six now. I dropped my bucket at about half past five; the adrenaline rush from that experience ensured that sleep was no longer an option.

It's been the week of the annual general meetings. We sat formally in Harlton Village Hall and Great Eversden Church ticking off the agenda. George has bowed out. He was churchwarden in Harlton for twenty-seven years – we will not see his like again. The casualty of this endless process and administration – PCC meetings, annual meetings, fundraising committees, worship groups, outreach groups, deanery synods, chapter meetings – has been an erosion of pastoral care on a grand scale. It has happened silently, slipping further and further away as another parish is added to a group, or two become three. This erosion of pastoral contact, almost

incidental contact, has perhaps defined more than anything
else the disconnection from the church that has taken place
over the last forty years. It has meant that we have become
distant, disconnected. The general line is we are 'out of
touch'; that is exactly what we are. The demands to keep the
show on the road, the loading of extra parishes and in many
cases more and more diocesan posts to go with them – youth
adviser, education officer, liturgical committee member, the
list is endless – has meant in reality less and less care on the
ground. It is that care, that contact that is missing and the
result has been a church that is quite clearly dislocated, distant
from society. Is it any wonder then that we are seen as 'civic
functionaries' before we are seen as priests? The fact is that
most people from outside the church still think we only work
one day a week.

This surrender to function, to process, has also elevated
those who are good at it, those who play the game. I have
been told on a number of occasions that I am not seen often
enough at all the official gatherings I am supposed to be at,
that if I want a diocesan job, preferment, promotion, whatever
you like to call it, then I really must make more effort on that
front. While I understand the realism, and that the advice was
well intentioned, I am not prepared to make a career out of
it, and I would say to those that do, that they do so at the
expense of their parishes and the church. The whole thing
needs turning upside down; there is a desperate and urgent
need that we realise the pastoral rather than the political,
that the solution to our current problems lies in love, not in
strategy. It is not something that involves churchmanship –
Evangelical, Charismatic, Liberal, whatever – the defence and
maintenance of those labels has cost us too much. It is not the
system of management that will resolve any of this, Synods,
PCCs, whatever. It is our whole approach to being priests and

what that actually means. If anything the only way forward is to let go of all the process and the practical; it is drowning us. We must also give up our careers, our own ambitions, our positions, be brave enough to be unimportant, to become servants, to become weak, to become vulnerable. We need to go the whole way. I know that now.

The Arbory Trust is on the launch pad. We met some representatives from Barton Parish Council last night in the vicarage in Barton. We told them that the chosen site was a forty-acre plot at the end of the village. Their main concern was coping with massive demand. This hasn't been something we've seriously considered. They were keen that we should try to make the woodland welcoming to the locals.

I hadn't realised that the last row of cottages before you leave the village is set aside for retired gardeners; what a wonderful idea. There are homes for retired priests – there is one in Dormansland in Surrey. It's at the bottom of the hill near the station. I used to pass it a lot; they all looked bald at the time. Some of them would come and preach at the church when the vicar was on holiday. One of them started off on the Sermon on the Mount and somehow ended up in Margate talking about donkeys. I think most of the congregation realised that it had all gone horribly pear-shaped before he did. He rescued himself gracefully, he seemed to literally run out of petrol stuttering to an almost silent ending. He then took off his glasses, announced in a warm Charlston voice that he had lost his thread, then turned and sat down. There is something about that space in churches, the colours they hide, that come cascading in when the sun shines. The freelance vicar in last week's *Church Times* accused the church of creating children out of adults, of locking us all into a never-never land. Children see more of vicars than adults do, they are frogmarched around formal religion, they are better equipped to believe in heaven than I am. Yes, we probably want that silver-lined certainty but as adults we can't have it; it's because we can't have it that we have to engage in looking for it. I'm not sure children are given that choice.

The bishop has resigned. He's going back to Durham to be principal of St John's College. His job is to inspire and educate those training to be priests. He inspired and educated me; he was a man of generous grace, someone who never seemed to be in a hurry, someone who always left you feeling better able to deal with the ragged edges of your soul. Someone who believes in mystery.

It's cold; the east wind has returned, burning the tops of the potato shoots and scalding the cherry blossom, leaving spilt tea on the petals. The summer is longer in coming and is usually spent like holiday money, days taken up with forgetfulness.

I still cannot shake it, this vision of living out for some time. It's very explicit, spiced with dreams of shells and shingle, dirt and dust: the idea, the notion to live off God. I'm supposed to be doing it now, of course, and it is harder with possessions and rotas. Imagine having nothing except what you could fit into your pockets. One pocket: you'd have to have a Bible in the other. Go with the gulls for six months, sleep in the woods, the castles of creation.

The problem with the parish system is the amount of energy required to keep it going; it has become self-centred, self-obsessed, moulding puppets out of priests. There is God but he/she is out on the edges of it all. We have placed ourselves at the centre, the resurrection is about living, not dying. The Te Deum, sung by twenty people who can't sing, is tedious in the extreme. Ireland on Wednesday, seventy-eight quid return to Kerry with car hire thrown in. We stay somewhere cheap and amble up the Macgillycuddy Reeks. I've never been before – my only worry is that I'll be disappointed. I hope it rains. Sarah has gone to Australia for five weeks; it will be meaner without her here.

It rained. It rained most of the time actually. The mountains are green up to the rock line; they are huge sponges. Everything drips. There is water everywhere – in pools, in lochs, in streams and rivers. The moss in places was six inches thick. On the first day we scrambled up Tommy's Mountain; it was cold at the top, the weather was erratic, snowing one minute with huge flames of sunshine the next. From the Macgillycuddy Reeks you can see the Atlantic. On the last day my knee gave out. On the top of Borah there is a false summit; we convinced ourselves we weren't on it and sat for lunch hunched in a shelter the size of a washing machine, the rain dripping through the rock-piled roof. The others went on to Carontouhill. We'd seen it briefly the day before, there was a cross up on the top. Three of us hobbled down into a loch-bottomed valley, the clouds sitting about two hundred feet above us; it was an extraordinary sight, the green sides of the mountains cut with streams enclosed under a white moving roof. The river that came off the loch had shattered into a hundred channels. Dippers shot across, moving low and fast; you could not have seen any of it and come away the same.

On the last morning we went out to the sea, a long stretch of sand leading outwards in front of a wall of dunes; the clouds were filling the horizon. We watched gannets bombing the water before we set off back to Killarney. Now there's a town, pubs everywhere. I'd made the fundamental mistake of assuming this was wild England with a different accent and better Guinness. It takes about three days before you fully comprehend you are in a different country completely. There is a melancholy about Ireland, but you blend that with the beauty, energy and innocence and you end up swallowing the diamonds shimmering in the rivers.

There was a girl in the lay-by on the road. She was standing next to an old man and a donkey with a double basket on its back. She was still there when we passed her again three hours later. She was there for the tourists to take her face back home. You don't do that unless you need the money, not on a cold April morning. The poverty must have been awful; it's there in the cracks of the old man's shoes and the ruins of the two-room crofts which had been replaced by Mediterranean breezeblock bungalows. The Rowan Tree pub in Glencar has a very comfortable windowseat; you could grow old gracefully there. I miss home though, I always miss it when I'm away. I miss being there, I always miss my family. Churches are such certain places, they are so rich, their bricks get into your bones.

However nasty people are to you, and some people can be mainly because they are in pain themselves, as a priest you can't turn round and say go and boil your head, you can't return abuse with abuse, you have to take it and walk it off perhaps, or aim it at God, hang it on the cross. It's something you get used to, you have to be a punchbag.

Apparently there is a WI calendar where the ladies have dispensed with their clothes; Pat brought it for us to have a look at. I got confused and asked everyone if they'd seen the Mothers' Union calendar. There must have been twenty people scattered on faulty chairs; the predominant colour was grey. Maybe in little places little things matter, you begin to notice the individual blades of grass. As a vicar you join the fabric of the place, there's no opt-out, your trade is other people's lives; you get to sense what they put on their toast. The age of the church is important here. A simple head-count in most country churches will tell you that in twenty years, and definitely thirty, they will all be gone, gone as they are now. This will be interpreted as the death of God. The system and the institution are fraying at the edges as humanity continues to privatise wisdom, love, humility and grace. All that's happening is that human beings in the West are saying to God, I don't need you, I do not want to be made uncomfortable by your insistence that I am holy. If I need miracles, I'll turn on to science – and as long as scientists are content to patent God's handiwork, who can blame them?

Most church services are cultural anathema, utterly alien to the way we express ourselves. The church must be the only institution still using seventeenth-century operating manuals and singing the hits of the 1860s. It's very simple really; change or die. We are heading for the wilderness, there is no doubt about it. The irony is we could have chosen it at least, maybe it's been chosen already. We can stand out there and shout at each other about sex and divorce, about incense and scripture, Rome or Canterbury, we can write our theology on stones. We can revel in the fact that we are a remnant. What point have we been proving? What have we been communicating, while science has been splitting atoms and undoing genes, showing us the insides of stars; while seventeen-year-olds have been scratching vinyl and doing E; while the global business community has been dining out on all of this? We have been swallowing starch, looking for solutions to our own problems and bowing to a medieval king. Where is our heart, where has our heart gone? Is it still beating?

The last two days have contained summer. The dusk has been a rich oil and the cow parsley is high, fermenting an easy laziness. The Orange Tips have emerged, going where they will. The robin is back in the scullery, I can't tell whether it's a male or female; we feed it bread and it's been following me around the garden coming up to my hand, dining on worms. It must have a nest close by. It's filling its beak and darting over the wall where the vegetable garden is.

Everything is now in: the runner beans, the lettuce, radishes, cabbages, sprouting broccoli, parsnips. I've re-sown the carrots. The first sowing produced about three seedlings from four hundred seeds. There is a real guilt that comes with the summer; the winter is easier. All I tend to do is work, but when you stop you realise it's never-ending. I should be visiting, consoling, planning, praying. There is no end to it, there is no natural lull; you could do sixteen hours a day every day of the week and because it's haphazard, reactive, you could immerse yourself in it, lose yourself. Perhaps that is what we should be doing.

Gore Vidal was in storming form last night. He ripped the whole lot to shreds, tore it to pieces, wiped the floor with the Oxford Regius Professor of Divinity. I agree with him: the notion of a God who allows evil and then condemns us for succumbing to it is not pretty. Also the idea of a blissful afterlife is all well and good, but if this is only available to those who behave themselves we're being blackmailed into heaven. Logically he's right. The trouble is we have spent so much time defending our faith, maintaining it, saving ourselves, that really there has been little evolution. Personal growth tends to follow a set of pre-ordained notches; Jacob's ladder must be pretty worn by now. I can agree with Gore Vidal completely, but it doesn't dent at all my complete belief that you and I are loved, that creation is divine, that the universe has purpose beyond admiration.

Christianity has stuck to the same script. We seem to have reached the point where the world has been christianised and we are left watching the dust settle while our scholars re-write the same thesis again and again and are intellectually martyred by the same old flaws in the argument. Jonson has a book about castles, explaining the ramparts, the chapels and the dungeons, what the soldiers wore. As it says, once cannons were developed, castles became unviable; they couldn't offer protection any more, they became redundant as human beings invented more effective ways of destroying them. Christianity has stayed in its castles. We have made this possible by calling them sacred, by consecrating them; we are now in the position of defending them. Worst of all we've been locked inside. The old stones are gracious but they were built around a set of certainties that no longer exist, the idea of church is actually quite different from the ambition that built them. Surely you can have a church that meets on a bench, on a mountain, in a nightclub. An organisation can be a church, a business can be a church, a football team can be a church, a charity can be a church, a group of itinerant silent monks can be a church. Who is the service for? Yes some people are called to be priests but in all honesty the one jacket doesn't fit everybody, the one job description is a nonsense really.

The bright-eyed theological student arrived this morning. Her thesis was conflict. I still have Gore Vidal's slow tones rewinding. I scored highly on the collaborative ministry front, the flat management model. Apparently other priests she saw lost too many points for avoiding confrontation, which explains her enthusiasm for our confrontationally coloured kitchen. She had a face that seemed dusted in flour with the sky in her eyes. You don't get schooled in confrontation but it is the stock in trade of every priest, and so it should be. I wish we could hear Lord Runcie's sermon after the Falklands War again: war, he said, was a sign of human failure. Mrs Thatcher according to the *Sunday Times* is apparently drinking more than she should; probably needed a large gin after that one. The Church of England stands resolutely against conflict. There seems to be an overriding obsession to please, not to offend anyone – we have become soulless and saltless in the process. We are playing politicians' cards, but we are not politicians, we are priests; we govern nothing. This need to be reasonable, accommodating is dished out by the Crown Appointments Commission in grey tones, guaranteeing the underlying underachievement of the Church of England. Jesus Christ did not avoid conflict, he actually embraced it. He understood more than anyone that, by saying materialism, greed and sexual excess would not help you recognise how much you are loved by God, he would incur the wrath of those who were addicted to them. He left us with a blueprint for dealing with the conflict that will quite naturally arise when you stand up and say what he said: Love your neighbour as yourself; turn the other cheek; do unto others as you would have them do unto you; love your enemies, do not curse them. The creative tension between church and society is probably at an all-time low.

The bank are squeezing us again. It hurts. I can't believe I was so stupid over the whole credit-card issue. It's not a credit card at all, it's a debt card; you are buying debt, your own. There was some very young voice on the phone shouting that the account had been overdrawn for three months. We have a far more glamorous financial heritage than that – we have been overdrawn for six years since I was a curate. We were in credit once for four days. To start chirping on about the fact that we have been overdrawn for three months really means he was either put up to it, following procedure, or was born yesterday. Overdrafts, he told me, could no longer be agreed by an account manager. They had to be run up the line. What this means is that you never actually get to talk to the person making the decision; this edict happened in a dark room far away from here. We are all apparently just expected to agree to this. The overdraft has been greater without concern and worry – it's actually just come down. If only they could see the struggle we go through. Today we are dogs.

The Churches Advertising Network is planning big things for the millennium. We agreed the theology: 'All you need is love.' The Jerusalem Trust also put their head round the door and a bloke who was described as a razor blade in cotton wool turned up. We're going to be producing two radio commercials and a cinema commercial, perhaps. How this is going to happen is still a little unclear. We'll be trawling for favours I think, not an ideal way to move forward, but financially we are left with no choice. The bank balance after the Easter campaign starts at around six and a half thousand pounds in credit, which in real advertising terms would just about buy you a quarter page in the *Daily Mail*. We shouldn't be doing this, flogging Jesus, not on our own. The Bishop of Wakefield, who is the communications adviser to the House of Bishops, at least is consistent; he consistently rubbishes most of what we do. There were supposed to be two new members joining us at the meeting, but they have been barred by their bishops, archdeacons, whoever they are. They were told, apparently, that we were too controversial. When you are ordained you have to make promises to be faithful to the bishop ordaining you. There is a huge tension between keeping them and enforcing them; you walk on barbed wire really. The confusion resides at the place where your role is determined and the criteria that define it. You see, it's not the money, because there is none. There is no real measure of success beyond the real and touching accolades of the people you serve, other than the accolades of your peers. I have heard too many excuses as to why someone didn't make bishop; they are tragic, all of them. To be a priest is enough surely, more than enough, there is no greater privilege I know. The lilac is out. It's the Clergy Conference tomorrow; a heady mixture of wolves and lambs all wearing each other's clothes.

The wallpaper in my room has seen better days, it's all right in patches but there is a time when it would have graced an Indian restaurant. The carpet is from the seventies; it must have come from an office or a betting shop, small black squares with various shades of orange. There's a bit of shag left on the pile under the sink, the rest of it has been well and truly flattened.

Either there is a bull in the room next door calling for a mate or the occupant is warming up for the world's snoring championships. Supper was a sort of recycled beef; I'm not sure that any of the meat was actually straight meat or any of the meal was actually straight food. The potatoes looked as if they'd been machine made, the cauliflower had definitely been killed and someone had drilled for the gravy.

None of this got us off to a good start. I bolted when I saw everyone sitting in the main meeting area, rolled a quick smoke and went outside. It was dark. I'd just sat down on the bench, when I heard the door opening behind me, there were footsteps on the gravel, then somebody stood still and broke wind very, very loudly indeed. At that moment the security lights went on. Neither of us spoke; we just pretended it hadn't happened.

We had Lavinia Byrne on earlier raving about the internet. She said that the best communication, that the fruit of communication, was to build community. There are some fine people here, genuinely good people; we're just not very good at mixing it. We're all right when we're in costume I'm sure, but thankfully once we are out of the role most of us flounder. I'm not sure how much we are meant to love each other – whatever that means – although I know it matters. Help me.

Tom Wright has just blown my mind, burnt my heart, what's left of it. He rode the same path as Philip Yancey in his book *The Jesus You Never Knew*. They both discussed the Sermon on the Mount, the Beatitudes; when these are translated, when they are stripped down into the present, you are taken into another world. It is impossible to take statements conceived in eternity and reduce them down to a user's guide; you cannot live in the foundations of a house. The line 'blessed are the meek for they shall inherit the earth' is a seed, the flowers that it grows are different in each generation. That in itself is a miracle. We have made the mistake, I make the mistake, of underestimating these words every day. To spout them does no justice either. We are not meant to use them, they are not meant as a retort or a last word – they are meant as the first word, they are meant to use us.

Possibly the best sentence in the ordination vows that every vicar takes is a promise that they 'speak afresh the words of the Bible in each generation, into each generation'. We cannot therefore take the old words, the old meaning and expect it to resonate now. All they leave is a faint echo of what they were. It is another language from another time. God is surely not static. The wonderful thing about religious traditions is the history they give us, the hindsight they allow us: the Gnostics, the

Benedictines, the forgotten Fathers who thankfully have left nothing of themselves in the desert. Each of us surely is a new creation – the choices we make are unique to ourselves. Too many times we're forced into other people's clothes. It's easier and requires less effort, but we are hiding really, hiding behind them: St Francis, Malcolm McLaren, Armani, Bruce Oldfield. We don't share ourselves, our souls, we hardly ever dare show our souls. Show love in any boardroom and you'll have your tongue ripped out. One of the biggest lies in our society is the lie of service. The supermarkets lick us, the multinationals are not actually doing anything for us – they are at best doing what they do on our behalf. They're not doing what they're doing for you, for me, they're doing it for themselves; there is absolutely nothing altruistic there at all. The whole thing is fuelled by personal ambition and personal insecurity.

Will Hutton spoke to us last night, he's the editor of the *Observer*. He outlined six contemporary revelations for us. He is genuinely moved by the rising inequality which it seems is necessary for the functioning and funding of a competitive world. He said as far as products were concerned we have a global glut, too much of too much: with cheap labour clamouring for work, production costs have actually come down in real terms. Companies in the West increasingly outsource much of their production to poorer places which pay poorer wages. He *didn't* say that the glut was the result of gluttony. He ripped into contemporary politicians for being spineless; he didn't say why they behaved in this way. Some of it surely has to do with the fact that any politician who bears this spine has it surgically removed by the national press which Hutton represents. He was the drunk driver standing there barracking his victim for not being able to walk. He has immense charisma; we forgave him for being late which, as we said, must have been something from 150 vicars. He is the fortuneteller; he just about asked us to pick a card and when we did he told us what it all meant. Like most powerful men he appeals to your vanity, scorches your sense of self. He rubbed chilli on our tongues and put onions in our eyes. It seems as if we are all heading for social meltdown, that the future had walls around it guarding luxury and imprisoning poverty behind airline posters promising palms and paw-paw. Yes, he had a dream, but it never stopped, it's never-ending: the constant promise of being millionaires or the potential to become millionaires; but those who fail will keep those who don't. Tom Wright saw this failure as success. Yes, blessed are the poor, the unemployed, the marginalised, for they can see God. Sing it.

The entertainment was in reverse drive. It all started well enough. The Bishop of Grunty Fen entertained the packed hall with a theological rendering of 'Mary, Mary quite contrary'. It looked as if the Archdeacon of Huntingdon was going to have an immediate coronary, he was laughing so much – he clearly didn't have time to draw breath. They sang to the bishop at the end. He was moved into the front row where he had to endure a shaky version of 'Mr Wonderful'. We've all been told to be visible on the night of the millennium, to be seen; we don't seem to have moved beyond first base here. What are we doing on New Year's Eve? Are we drinking to his death, his poverty, his insistence that we turn the other cheek, his way of seeing, his way of being? I thought the sharp edges would fade; they can become smooth all too easily, ground into a reasonable surface. You trade your razor blades for pumice and there it stops. Tom Wright read beautifully but he looked at us very quizzically when he told us we were the salt of the earth and the salt has lost its taste. As priests we generally only tend to go so far. God offers us so much, but we seem to accept so little.

The spring has turned vivid, angelica up at shoulder height, the robins are feeding their young; they're in the kitchen now, stealing crumbs. The trees are heavy with new leaves and the buttercups blaze. There's bad feeling back at the ranch. A friend of ours has offered us all a holiday, a week in Corsica. He offered to pay for the flight, the car hire and the accommodation. The week takes in the beginning of the flower festival and the village service on Sunday. I won't be here for either. It's not good for the guilt, being a callous bastard. I've never felt guilt before, not guilt like this; it's made of lead. The trouble is there is always so much more you can do, there is always someone else to see, more to be organised. The guilt when you sit down is awful, letting your hair down is almost impossible. It's not the faith, not the certainty that life is holy, that every atom is blessed, that within the words of Christ, however few we have, is divine love, divine knowledge, divine imagination. You commit yourself to failure, you see; your faults become public property, you become public property. You give up living for yourself. This is right, there can be no other way. But what keeps the church alive is very different from what keeps a marriage alive. Who comes first – your children or the congregation? It's the same in contemporary life – it's a constant tension – who do you die for? I know I ought to be here and I can understand the whispers will say, Why fly then, and they are right. They are right because it is important; it may only be a flower festival and one service but it's very important here. That in itself is good. But you are torn down the line where friendships and family are concerned. There are no clean edges. There is terrible guilt because looking back there I was in Rome, in the south of France, Durham, Norfolk, Ireland; this bloke is living off Reilly and here he is, swanning off to Corsica. Even worse, the only one that I paid for out of all of them was Ireland, the rest were all bought for me. But there's a high price for it. I haven't travelled so much in years but always there is the feeling that I shouldn't, that I should stay at home, be there, try to love – not because I'm so arrogant that I believe I'm needed, but because I don't want to let people down. I genuinely want to help, to heal, to give, but that works on 360 degrees: dividing it out is awful. It's not something that you can have time off from. The whole idea of a day off, which they've now called a rest day, is a contradiction in terms. So often it's there that you are able to make peace to reconcile yourself to God. Don't think that priests believe all the time or, come to that, are aware of God 100 per cent of the time – we are not. I would imagine Christ was the only person who was aware of God 100 per cent of the time. We're not that strong, any of us, we're simply not able to do it, though we'd like to.

May

The moon is down to a single curved line. It's not dark now – the sky has summer in it. The road down through Newton comes up a hill; there are not many in Cambridgeshire. The clouds were banked up black, making mountains on the horizon, and above them in that thin eternal blue we get at dusk was this new moon. Strangely you could see it all in recess behind its luminous edge. The Celts had thin places where the gap between God and human beings was vulnerable, a clear sense of 'through the glass darkly'. We have a grand God really. He has big hands, big hair – we do not see this God as delicate at all. Modelled on power, muddled by desire, we go for the wide-screen version every time. Theologians perhaps give us detail but they are dealing with the individual hairs on a paintbrush, trying to describe them, separate them. We get tangled up in words: it's easy to distil religion into essential politics, to cram faith into justice, to say we have a green God, to declare the purpose of hell, the brilliance of love. This distillation in fact reduces God to digestible units. God becomes virtual, the words of Christ an anthem for the poor, the broken. But what we are doing really is trading surround sound for mono. What was incredible about Rome was the sense that it is a place that wrestles with all of it. The dove in the window at the front of St Peter's was sublime because at the end of it all, at the beginning as well, it declared that you are spiritual and God deals with you, loves you on this level.

What is being healed if you are in pain? I have no doubt that physical healing happens, but the real healing is spiritual always. Maybe that is why priests are broken people: we are, all of us. Some of us hide it better than others. A calling in that sense is also a healing. It is a recognition of brokenness. I find we still teeter on that edge and it's true we are neither really in the world nor out of it. What was interesting about the conference was that, despite all the talking up that went on in the best spin traditions, we are increasingly a besieged minority in an ever more hostile climate. We have lost the protection of tradition, we have become the embarrassing guest at consumer society's table and far from being confident and self-assured we are increasingly ridiculed and obviously broken. This has to be the best position we've found ourselves in in years.

We have run out of thread with the bank. Our cheques have taken on a rubbery quality; they've been busy bouncing this and that. No more favours on that front I fear. It's been a hell of a week really. I've been called irresponsible, self-seeking, reckless, lacking in moral fibre, unable to take the flak; I have been told I dress like a tramp. I have been sworn at, lied to, denigrated and stitched up and all this by a small minority who call themselves church-going Christians. You expect the pettiness that comes with living in any goldfish bowl; the ruddy great faults are fine, we all have them. What is hard is the nastiness, the spite. I wasn't prepared for it. I wanted to believe that kindness and love were the stock-in-trade of those who attend church – most of them fly that flag. Layla called this morning. She said she woke up with Jeremiah 4:3, she didn't know what it said but apparently I had to read it: 'For thus says the Lord to the people of Judah and to the inhabitants of Jerusalem, break up your fallow ground and do not sow among thorns.' Well, it would seem this course of action isn't going down at all well with a handful of old sods.

I'm on the net, emails have been firing in. In this diocese the communications director has set up the system whereby us religious types can talk shop. Today it's universal primacy, in normal language the debate is about whether it's possible to have one head of the church, that is, the pope. Is this the beginning of a well-known corporate strategy of merging and selling, downgrading and rationalising? The Seventh Day Adventists are having none of it. They point out there is nothing biblical about universal primacy. The Anglicans are fighting back with the comment that there is nothing biblical about church structures. We should soon, I think, reach the startling conclusion that there is nothing biblical about going to an Anglican church. Maybe the Seventh Day Adventists have got there before us. What on earth do we do then? Tonight we're going to eat the first of our lettuces. Out of the ground, quick wash, splash of dressing, lovely.

You can't actually go away without unplumbing the proverbial kitchen sink and dispensing bits of it to all and sundry. She who vamped the bishop at the clergy conference is taking the services on Sunday, twenty quid a hit. She should charge more really, I think. On Tuesday morning Edward the churchwarden is taking morning prayer. The Wednesday morning communion has been rescued by a non-stipendiary minister who, by all accounts, is booked up every Sunday until September. Next Sunday the Methodist minister is leading the joint service and the ex-rural dean is at Harlton for eleven o'clock. Plus there's someone who's coming in to feed the mice, someone else is kindly watering the vegetables – this has been a military operation. A whole lot of stuff came through this morning on 'post millennium': 'how to build a new church for the new century'. Since I've been ordained we've had the year of the small parish, the year of stewardship and this is the pre-millennium year, then the millennium, and now building a new church for the new century. I would very much like to have a year of contemplation, followed by a year of prayer. Layla sent me a wonderful tape, an evangelist spilling honey. He said that when we speak ill of people we curse them. Conversely we bless them by speaking well of them. He was speaking to a group of people in Horsham: 'We're gonna bless Horsham, Alleluia!' in tones that sat between a DJ and a politician. I can't work out where the line between entertainment and charismatic experience is. You could read his highs; they weren't so much scripted but they came at you and hit you on cue. Do you find God or does God find you? The church tends to present God with as much subtlety as MacDonalds. We tell people what God is, we dictate his purpose, but we don't teach people to look, to listen – we don't invite them into the empty spaces of their souls. We give them answers not questions; we save them without ever considering how they in fact continually save us. We tell them that money is worthless – it is – and then we turn round and say how important it is that they should give as much of it as possible to us. The strategy, if there has been such a thing, seems to have revolved around maintaining the network, our presence on the ground. To say that it's cast around maintaining a tradition would be over-gilding it. But there is no doubt that it is how it comes across. You could say that in the fight to keep breathing our efforts have largely been consumed by the practical rather than the spiritual. We have opted for the bricks rather than the mortar. Corsica tomorrow.

There is something about mountains – each one of them is different. From a distance they seem as one: crammed together, defining God's sky, calling you perhaps. We walked for four hours through wild thyme and lavender along a narrow path that hid the heat in its shade. Ten minutes in and there was nothing: not a building, not a telegraph pole, no droning cars. We eventually followed this valley upwards through the pine trees by the end. Once we were above the tree line it became very hard. In front of us, all the way in this rolling heat, was this brown ridge, splattered with snow patches. We settled for an hour or so at the refuge hut, dumped our packs, and then climbed the 700 metres to the top, walking across some of the snowfields to get there. It took us about two hours. There was a concrete cross at the top with weathered corners, consecrated by the Bishop of Adjacio in 1947. Was he really needed up here in all this radiant emptiness? I'm not sure he was. The colours, when the evening came, were set to a different score. We so lightly call it blue; there must have been an infinite number of blues – maybe we notice them more if we haven't seen them before. It was all silent, completely silent. Napoleon described Corsica as an excrement; Corsicans have described him in equivalent terms. It has been hewn out of poverty. In the past I'm sure it kept the richest thieves in the world, but now as Europe becomes swallowed in smart buttons it is fantastically untidy and wildly expensive at the same time; the bandits have saved it from respectability and the mountains have no purpose other than their own.

We're back. The flower festival was in full swing today, the tired walls wilting under the resonance of buckets of colour. The music was improvised, sometimes piano, sometimes choir, sometimes the violin. It was the first time that there seemed to be an unstructured joy. At one point one of the choir started singing as they sat together at the back drinking the customary tea. The whole experience seemed to be liberating. So much is structured – everything we seem to do is riddled with rights and rules about rules. Surely none of them matter more than the reality of love, the presence and power of God's love. In too many instances the interpretation of that love has been constricting. It has, despite the best attempts of Protestantism, actually been standardised by it. In the escape from Catholicism the church, in cahoots with the Crown, simply re-created the rule book. It probably seemed at the time as if it was being thrown away; it wasn't, it was simply being redrafted. This has atrophied in the lino of Church House and clearly is responsible for the consistent underperformance of the Church Commissioners. The weight of this wears heavy. As a priest you carry it on your back – you have to be strong, not to let it weigh you down. Sarah is home, maybe that's why everything feels better. I remember once sitting in this room. It was full of books and the director of ordinands let me smoke, which in retrospect was very kind of him. He sat there listening intently as I tried to explain why I felt that God was breathing down my neck. We talked about worship. I arrogantly said I thought it was theatre. He agreed. Perhaps it is – the mistake though is to become an actor. If there is such a thing as a calling, of which I have no doubt, then the only way to make any sense of it is to reconcile yourself to the dreadful realisation that God has called you and it's you that he wants, she wants, not some actor hamming up history. It's quarter to ten now, but it's still light. There is a field down by the river in Harston, it's small; it has huge chestnuts hanging over the edges. There, *there* is the flower festival: it's free, have you seen it?

The ad for the millennium is a recreation of the Last Supper. Sitting round Christ are executives from the twelve major world corporations: MacDonalds, Microsoft, the usual suspects. It's brash and bold. I'm not sure it has the spark of the revolution poster, but it is a start. The line running across the top reads, 'All you need is love.' It struck me when the line was being explained that the Church of England seems to have lost the ability to communicate basic Christian truth. Awesome statements such as 'love the Lord your God with all your heart, with all your soul, with all your strength' have been dissected by theology and cracked into a thousand different pieces. Christianity has become a religion of the mind; you need a degree to understand it. We have turned the parables into tomes. The good news has collapsed into a late-night discussion programme on what that statement actually means. One thing is for sure – we don't treat it as news. It has become theology, it has become the currency of the temple, it has become liturgy, dogma. It was given as love, grace, as truth, as the knowing become known. We are called to live it, not to log it. Our theology has really become a hard shell around our faith; we have been seduced apparently by our own reflection here. We surely must live our faith to learn it, rather than learn it to live it.

June ·

The Strawberry Fair was grunge and glitter, 50,000 people drinking, dancing, looking. Hair of every conceivable colour, beer and bangles, the music changing every twenty metres, food from every corner of the world served in rank plastic eaten in the rain, the air filled with joss-sticks and hash. The faces were young in the main; the travellers would just sit where they were, claim some space and settle in. The Mohawks and dreadlocks muddied the edges of gender. This was a tribe that the interest rates don't touch, the festival summer caravan rolling all over England. The next stop was in Wimborne in Dorset. Most of the pitches sold unbleached, natural, organic. From here you could save the world from itself. Thank God some people are still dreaming and are prepared to reject respectability, to be rejected, to die dirty. The people that run it are mostly Buddhists, kind with honest eyes. I volunteered: from six o'clock onwards I got the lost children, dogs, and people too off their face to know who it belongs to. I stopped for ten minutes and grabbed a bite to eat, picked up some worn prayerbooks on one of the stalls. I asked how much they were and the man said I could have them. 'I leave them out, I don't sell them,' he said, 'they are too precious for that. They turn up sometimes and I just give them away.'

There is an interesting line between being off your face and being in touch. The line is that soft drugs, hard drugs, raise your level of consciousness, that the vale is scratched between here and Nirvana, that you become part of a raised spiritual experience. You don't. It's your soul dying – you are numbed from the pain of it as it pleads with you for reality. And you are given a period of oblivion from the crippling loneliness that chews up your words and pins you on the membrane of your most vulnerable sense. When the gap between reality and your own release from it goes beyond the critical point you become an addict. We are all addicts of something – most of us hide our addictions behind our eyes. But when the addiction becomes external to yourself then surely you are split by it. You will fight a dirty war to become whole again. Not everyone is cut out for the mainstream, why should they be? Churches are full of people who exist on the edges of society. That is not such a bad thing either. But we tend to minister to one tribe in a number of different ways. We need to get out there more. The chances are that if you built your cardboard cathedral here and if you went by the order of service you would end up with a few carbon copies. We need to be more daring than that. While we quibble endlessly over incense and scripture and the universal church we are missing the point. These people aren't going to go to church, they're not going to settle into a parish and support that structure. Perhaps it's not what they're called to do; anyway we need their thorns in us. We've got to loosen up a bit here – all you need is a tent and a stove. Imagine, what is a priest anyway?

The Family Service was good; it wasn't packed but there was a real sense of God reaching for all of us. We looked at the parable of the tares. It was Conservation Sunday; the children scattered wildflower seeds in the churchyard. There seems to have been a run on funerals – there are four over the next six days. The funeral this afternoon was clear and kind. We had some Peter Tosh in the middle and, at the end while the coffin was being carried out, the reggae song sounded fantastic, seeping into the old walls. The church was full of 150 faces who came to mourn a gentle man; there are far too few of them.

There were twenty-three of us in Harlton on Sunday. I have to write the numbers down at the end of every service. The diocese use them to calculate money we should pay every year. There is a large amount of polythene in Harlton – it moves in the wind, weaves behind the leaded window that's being re-leaded. The summer's a good time, a time to breathe out, space from the rush of Advent, Christmas, Lent, Easter, Harvest. Once you pass Pentecost, there's generally clear water until Harvest, then Christmas looms. The first of the fêtes is on Saturday in the Eversdens. There was a little owl trapped in the church on Monday morning in Great Eversden; its wings seemed far too big for its body. They fly completely silently; it is as if they make no effort at all. The owl population has suffered more than most from the legalised ethnic cleansing that is being practised without remorse by modern agriculture. Farmland has become a wasteland, the killing fields of a so-called civilised society. If you kill the skylark's food, you kill the skylarks.

Genetic modification simply enshrines the right to rule in the same manner. We move further along the road of working against our environment rather than working with it. There can be nothing natural about it, because essentially it is opposed to what it finds in nature and the way it finds it. It is oppression of the worst kind. I accept that it is progress and that it does indeed present a brave new world, and all brave new worlds need pioneers. But human beings surely lost something when one man said to another, one woman to another, This is my tree, I own it. This territory issue has now gone beyond the field, the tree; it has become part of the very substance of that life. The charge of God's dominion has been interpreted as a licence to enslave the natural world; the process of genetic modification moves this further down the line. The patenting of genetic material common to all life, to all of us, is not only theft of the highest magnitude, it also perpetuates this enslavement model. The knowledge gained from it by the wealthy West will be used to further subjugate the Third World simply because it is based on ownership. We own it; they don't. Maybe this is a dying voice, but surely we must work with the natural world to give it space to sing on its own, on its own terms, not ours; be big enough not to want to control it; to work with it, not against it. Maybe this is indeed Adam's fruit: us having what we want, the way we want it, when we want it. We can dress it up and call it progress but it's actually about selling cheap food and, as the protagonists will tell us, feeding more human mouths. I used to think that this was, perhaps, a natural extension of human beings' dominion over nature. But it's obscene really how this new technology, if you can call it that, relies on what is a dangerous and outdated model of dominion: the control model, the model of master and slave. We unsurprisingly play the king in the castle, under the illusion that it's our God-given right. Yes, God has given us dominion, but the intructions he left were to till and care for the Garden of Eden. Perhaps we are reaching the point where we need to redefine our relationship with the environment. We need to do that urgently in so much as what has supposedly been done by modern agriculture is said to be done on my behalf for my benefit. I profoundly disagree. Perhaps in the industrialised urbanised West we have lost complete touch with the natural world; the fruits of the environmental crisis we face are grown there, maybe. We have lost any real sense of a personal relationship with the fields and the birds and thus we are essentially indifferent to them. The heady soup of the environmental movement draws us into battle on this front – it has become us and them. Maybe that is what it has boiled down to. I'm not so sure anymore.

An interesting letter arrived this morning from W. Larkins. It reads:

May we remind you that the lightning conductor system on your property is due for inspection to ensure its efficiency; it's a known fact that to have a faulty lightning conductor is worse than having no conductor at all.

I couldn't agree more.

The distance has gone quiet. The edge is set in uncertain layers struggling in a sombre dusk; it's cold, the air coming in from the north bruising the roses. Yesterday I put a net on the strawberries to try to protect them from the birds, they were gorging on anything pink. I shouldn't have done it; this morning the netting had been pulled up, almost rolled neatly. What was left of a wren was caught in the end – the cats next door had an easy kill. From the size of its wings I think it was a fledgling. It was thoughtless, I shouldn't have done it. The best way is to tie thread around the strawberries and hang silver paper off it, but as usual I didn't make the time, I went for the quick solution. There is always a cost.

My grandmother died last week. She was in her nineties. She was brought up by gardeners and nannies and had one of those wonderful voices that you don't find any more, an accent which is designed to beat the echo in the large rooms of country houses. Towards the end of her life she started to

give everything away and systematically let go of everything
she had. She followed Gurdjieff and had a spirituality that
recognised God in all forms and everything. She was a blue
domer. She could hear your heart. By the end of her life she was
blind and deaf. Mervyn Peake painted her when she was young
and clearly beautiful. The picture hangs in her sitting room,
which was emptier every time I saw her. She had impeccable
manners and knew how to hold a napkin, a meaningless grace
perhaps, but if it is done with grace it is a grace nonetheless.
You can eat chips and vinegar with grace.

Our church meetings in Haslingfield have become far more
relaxed. There is a good deal more laughter, dare I say it, and
they are really very much more enjoyable. It's the first of the
fêtes on Saturday. The bombing has stopped in Kosovo. Are
precision weapons meant to make us feel better about killing? I
have another funeral tomorrow. I've given up on days off – really
I should have done it earlier. This is not a job; to treat it as such
puts you and everyone else in an impossible position. It's a way
of life – it is genuinely a calling. I have to remember that.

It rained – it was like standing under a waterfall actually –
and it didn't stop. It relented once in a while but even that's
being generous. The Savoy Jazzmen were sublime. They kept
everything happy, but as fêtes go it was English all over. Rain,
tea, fabulous cakes, spot the chicken, put the ball in the ladder,
the book stall, home-made sweets, raffles, face painting: it was
all there. I must have been asked at least forty times whether
I could have a word with him upstairs about the weather. As
a family we probably spend somewhere between fifteen and
twenty quid at each one of these fêtes. Jonson won the golf,
but I have a feeling he was the only one under seven to play
it. India won the bar skittles, and by some fluke I won the ball

in the ladder and came away with two fine bottles of St Serre, some cricket pads for 50p, an English to Welsh dictionary, some scones that were left over, a lemon cake and a cucumber plant. It's difficult not to end up taking on Hugh Grant's mannerisms, stammering and struggling with words. You have to be erudite; you may want to disappear behind the barn and drink cider with the ducks but you can't, it's showtime.

I had to decline an invitation to the fête supper on the grounds that I have been out every night last week and that I wanted to spend an evening at home with Jacs and the children. I also took a lot on the chin for suggesting that we change the service times, perhaps do an evensong. The only other option is a service at eight o'clock in the morning, I don't mind that. Although I'm not convinced at all that eight o'clock in the morning is a good time to have a service – those days are gone, I think. I worked most of Friday and all of Saturday, today was completely jammed as well but I didn't make it to the countryside service at 4.30 this afternoon. There is always the problem of rationalisation – do you say to families that you only do baptisms on one Sunday and cram them all into one baptism service? It hasn't come to that yet. A lot of other people do it but you lose the intimacy and compromise people's freedom of expression; the whole thing ends up as some corporate dunking ritual.

If you met someone who was reliant on God it would be both threatening and frightening, I think. He must have been incredibly threatening, Jesus; he must have been considered dangerous. The Pharisees surely had their patch to defend like the rest of us, but to resort to what was effectively a corporate killing implies that they felt that everything they stood for was being undermined successfully. I'm not sure he was a victim; we might like to paint it that way but victims don't behave the way he did. Most of us lose our charm when we are threatened; he didn't.

It was hot today – the sun has a knife in it. The sky held half of the moon; you had to look for it though. You know how it is in the daytime, strange that something so apparently white can hide in all that blue. It was the school this morning, the question and answer session on what a vicar does. 'Why is it called the dog-collar?' 'How much do you get paid?' 'Do you believe everything in the Bible?' 'Do you ever cry at funerals?' 'What is it like working on Christmas Day?' 'Do you like some services more than others?' It was far more entertaining than last night, when the school governors took us millimetre by millimetre through the government's new home-school agreement policy. It was a death of sorts, being worn down and down by fashionable politics, slowly tied up in tape that did little more than encourage you to stop breathing altogether. I'm still trying to fathom whether there is any reward whatsoever attached to being a school governor. Should this purely be an act of penance, or are we caught up in some strange endurance gameshow where humour has been banned altogether? I also can't work out whether this is the type of situation that the Education Secretary desperately wants to reform or whether the reforms have already taken place.

The May Balls are on in Cambridge; the fireworks reach this far – low booms that begin around ten o'clock and have the echo of a distant war. The reciprocal sounds in Kosovo would not bring people out of their houses, they would force them into them. They say that a snake's venom heals as well as kills.

I'm sure God forgives us more easily, more readily, than

we forgive ourselves. The weight of narcissism, arrogance and selfishness rests heavy. As a priest your sins take on cinematic proportions. I'm sure we are wounded by sin, it weakens us. I can only say, looking at the way Christ responded to life – despite his protestations for the cup of suffering to be taken from him in the Garden of Gethsemane – that he was not weakened as we are, as I am. To have to withstand the adulation without becoming vain, to have taken on the suffering without becoming bitter, to have withstood the temptation without becoming proud, to have continued healing without becoming hardened to sickness, to have continued teaching without becoming impatient, each one of those perhaps has a hook of its own. But it would seem that he had no sin. The passages in Matthew where he rails against the Pharisees could be described as anger, vitriol even. But it was perhaps more passionate than anything else. He never pulled his punches but he never returned the punches he took either. Not one human being has come anywhere close to that. I'm not sure at all that this Anglican and Catholic obsession with the communion service is helping us. We remember his death at the expense of his life, we have isolated his words at the last supper, 'Do this in remembrance of me'; they have become, 'Do this in remembrance of this meal.' That is surely not what he meant.

What Jesus Christ did was to take God from the outward to the inward. From the outer life to the inner life, he returned God to us, to our souls, to the place where our battles are really fought, are being fought. So much of what he said was directed at our inner life, the life no one can see except God. It's a life we will have to account for, it is the person we really are. 'If you should even look at a woman lustfully then you are committing adultery': it's not that ridiculous, it's true. Our society does not recognise the inner life at all, the inner person, not until they need a hospital. Peace has become something that you can find in a hammock on the Caribbean, love has been defined by sex, truth by advertising. In the West we are physically fat but our inner selves are starving. Our greatest disease is loneliness. We are presented with a stream of distractions and, if we are lucky, we become numb, unfeeling, or, as Gurdjieff would say, we fall asleep lulled by the manufactured vision of a perfect consumer life which serves no one other than the manufacturers. There is no doubt the church got fat, we are better thin, in thin places. Perhaps we are in the desert now. Who will save us? That depends on who we accept water from.

We said farewell to my grandmother today in a small chapel outside Bath. The service was a mixture of tradition and radicalism which was exactly what she was. She wrote it all out before she died; we had the 23rd Psalm followed by some reflections from Buddha which could very well have been taken from the Sermon on the Mount. Is Allah the same as Yahweh, contemplation the same as prayer? It's an ancient ruse, my God is more powerful than your God: the Old Testament is full of it. Maybe it is our response to God that is different. To put them all in the same pot is fine, but though you may end up with faith it is a faith without religion, a walk without a way, it is a tasteless soup, a teaching without teachers. Worse still, it is self-justifying. Was Christ a guru? Yes – he spoke, he speaks, to your soul, the parables are soul food. He tried to tell us in all he said; everything he said was addressed to our souls. As priests, when we are instituted we are given 'the cure of souls', old charmed words, but that is what we are supposed to do. I have a feeling that if that is all we do then nothing else should concern us.

We seem to have pasteurised everything, our relationships

with creation have become rural mission. There are so many other quangos where we take a year to produce a sheet of A4 but they all really say the same whatever the subject matter boils down to, justifying their own existence. We end up mummifying ourselves, muttering to ourselves. The very existence of most of these bodies suggests that we have become lost in the corridors of an institution that is looking desperately for results to shore up its weaknesses. Maybe we should just be weak. At the last clergy conference but one this bishop stood up and spoke breathlessly and persuasively about getting involved in local government. I was very impressed at the time – he's very well thought of, apparently, might end up as the archbishop, some say – but now it seems awful, dreadful, there was no love in it. It was just another formula: the latest get-out-of-jail card, as we go round and round the board collecting the diminishing rent. We need the rent, I know that: it pays for the chicken on Sundays, the pints of glorious Regatta in the glorious Queen's Head, a fork to dig the garden, the carrot seeds, the purple paint. I was told the other day that church buildings have not been in such good repair for centuries. That's absolutely true, but it's not what we're about. Yes, we should make beautiful things but that's not really what we're here for, a celebration of plaster and paint, polished statues and clean linen. Has the church become bricks? Is that what we are giving the starving, the lame, the dispossessed: the living water poured into a cement mixer, gurus of girders?

The clouds are exquisite; last night they settled into long lines. Once the sun was behind the horizon it lit their edges yellow and orange before they burnt to pink and out into the gloaming. This evening there was layer upon layer, all the colour of eggs. This afternoon there was one immense cumulus, brilliant white, each curve illuminated by a fine silver line. I learned to watch the sky in the Fens. Up there there is only ten per cent land, the rest is heaven. It forces its way through the cuts in your skin, into your heart.

There was a lovely story today at the outreach meeting, another committee where we plan events; we ate German biscuits and drank English tea. The job of the outreach committee is to further good relations between the Methodists and the Anglicans; we've planned a picnic and a harvest supper. The chapel is booming really, which is good. It's a warm, comfortable, modern building with a hard floor. Hopefully next year we will have more services together. It seems a nonsense that both separate groups are trying to raise money to extend their premises when we are in fact no more than 100 metres apart. I like the Methodist minister immensely – he is a very diligent honourable man. We are separated by the need to maintain what we are individually responsible for. Essentially we are competitors, we have to survive; we waste too much energy doing it and we both know it. Anyway the story goes that after Terry Waite came back from the Lebanon the Queen gave him the use of Balmoral. Imagine you're the only person staying in a twenty-four-room hotel – wouldn't you be tempted to look through her sock drawers? Probably not, if you are Terry Waite. Apparently the Queen said he could ask whoever he wanted to stay with him so the Archbishop of Canterbury, who was Robert Runcie, came up for a couple of days. They were walking in the woods one afternoon when a local man saw them and went up to Terry Waite and said 'Are you Terry Waite?' Terry Waite said he was, and the local man said, 'I would be very pleased if you would come back to my home for a wee dram.' Then, looking over Terry Waite's shoulder in the direction of Robert Runcie, he said to him 'Ay, and you can bring your wee friend as well.'

I always thought the feminine form in its staggering beauty would gently decline, in the sense that as the grey hairs arrived the shock of the unfathomable beauty of a naked woman would diminish. You would be left with dusk, and the acidic discotheque lights of the past would become no more than an adolescent parody. I was not prepared for the fact that the mystery of femininity would deepen rather than unravel as it bangs up against ever more worn synapses.

From an academic standpoint the attractions of celibacy are plain, obvious: a life lived for God and no other. The New Testament especially has no sex in it – it's as if God has joined forces with Johnny Rotten and agreed that sex is no more than 'two minutes of squelching' and is really a rather unfortunate necessity of the human condition. Do the angels turn away? I don't know; it's what it feels like. I can only say that, as a heterosexual man, I am constantly struggling with the chaos on that front, the wolves lick the door. The desire to see, to touch, to kiss, these are fish in the water; sometimes they are near the surface, sometimes they are in the deeps. The temptation to fish is always there, to see how silver they are, but as a man you are generally left trying to contain a 5 kg fish on a 1 kg line. I read recently that your sexuality does horrible things in your imagination as you age, but, out of sight of the world, this old man was saying, these dreams turn sour. Marriage is all well and good but the landscape of our society is not marriage-friendly; as an institution it is looking decidedly dog-eared. The way in which marriage is expressed, the wooden boundaries around it are rotten. There are no role models to speak of – it seems paralysed in a glamourless pain. Your wedding certificate is a ticket to Middle England; when you have done your falling in love the romance is over and you are someone else and the photographer has done with you – you are on the other side of the door. But surely marriage is the cauldron of love;

it's where we learn to love, to take the roses and the razors as one. Maybe the boundaries should be moved. It seems desperate that you have to give up intimacy with members of the opposite sex, that real friendships free from sex should be considered dangerous rather than rich. Surely part of being a grown-up is that you set your own boundaries.

We launched our appeal in Haslingfield last night. About forty of us bounced around the village hall. I thought it was going to be slightly easier raising £200,000, but after the free wine and cheese no one actually had filled in a covenant form apart from yours truly; £194 a year, that's all. There are 1,600 people in this village; if 200 filled in the form that would be it. Everyone always says fundraising is torture. I'm looking forward to going to Harlton tomorrow, I don't know why. Stephen Sykes says that churches are sacred places set aside for God. Maybe they are the inner space of the community, the space where the inner life is brought to life. Maybe they turn us inside out – that's what they should do. Saints are perhaps people who reveal more of their soul than the rest of us.

We had rain today. The sky sank, bringing the sea in with it. You know how everything loses colour when it rains on the beach? Up on the Fens when it happens in winter you are cast into a black and white landscape: the black soil, the white sky. There were very few young people in Haslingfield today; the back of the church had a lot of holes in it, the front was almost full. Harlton was depleted. It didn't matter – it never does. The summer is always more settled. I love all these Pentecosts, a long line of Sundays that take us on to Pentecost 21 in September. Everything relaxes until Christmas, which starts at harvest festival really. The church should breathe out after the millennium, do nothing for a year. We should just be, listen, pray, be driven by nothing. Have nothing to achieve, no ambitions to meet, a year with God.

The documentary on St Paul's this evening was shocking. Endless discussions on who was going to stand where, east or west. The arrogance on display left you feeling as if you'd been forced to inhale mothballs.

The fact that there on film the young woman priest presided over a Eucharist and those who were celebrating with her refused to accept it, refused the body and the blood of Christ from her, was frankly unsurprising, other than it provided the first episode with its dreadful climax. The most pitiful sight of all was this woman preaching at the end to empty chairs. Here, in one of the greatest cathedrals in the world, the fruits of the current administration were there for all to see. St Paul's has become a cathedral consumed by concerts, strangled by chords that are played out as the canapés go round in well-heeled houses on Boxing Day – this is the dreadful present. Old men in old rooms are dredging through canon law to try to find a loophole big enough to accommodate their obese egos. It has become a function room, not a church, religion by numbers.

There are some days that you have to simply withdraw and give the emptiness to God. If you can do that, if you can let God fill the spaces, refill you, then you may survive. Too many people say they don't have enough time, that there are not enough hours in the day. Some have sold out to the structure. There is a structure: there are the deanery synods, the worship groups, the outreach groups, the school governors, the fundraising committee, the board of social responsibility, the houses committee and endless rounds of potentially endless meetings. They have claimed many lives – the synod dries slowly around you, the moss creeps into your paws. Yes God is rain, but in the end you don't notice it, you can't feel it. The temptation of course is to make yourself indispensable, needed. The more you are needed the less, it seems, you need God; you become strong, you don't become weak. The mechanisms of corruption are perhaps in-built into the church and if they weren't, there there would be others.

London was damp last night and strangely empty, there was nobody in Soho except a few boys begging under cold blankets, groups of prostitutes who were too young huddled together in doorways.

It was sum-grinding this afternoon: it happens at the same time every year, the half-hour slot with the clergy taxation services. They hire hotel lobbies or church halls, and you have to turn up with a year's worth of receipts, knowing exactly how many stamps you've bought over the last twelve months, how many biscuits were eaten by parishioners and how much your partner has spent on paint. For a priest, lighting and heating are tax-deductible; I'm not sure whether that's completely kosher in my case as I spend my days out in the shed. Our surplices are also tax-recognised, along with other items such as theological books, Bibles and gowns. We are a special case.

There is something profoundly melancholy that takes place when there is a permanent drizzle. The wonderful shadows are silenced and the birds are quiet. It is a quiet time, a space in summer's party when the usual music is switched off. Maybe that's what inspires our memories. The principles that allow memory to form are different for all of us I'm sure, although extreme emotional circumstances would seem to press the button that takes the picture we carry around with us. But there is another type of memory – the memories that come from a point of stillness, the time you were on your own as a child at the top of the house, or when you watch the plane fly over and there is only you, the memory that comes from the still centre. Most churches in the countryside have that still centre, have that stillness. They are not busy places. There can be no doubt we have less silence now: planes fly over, the radio goes, the washing machine, the taps running, traffic, lawnmowers. Imagine how quiet it must have been without them. Maybe that is what the desert gives, which is why it's so precious.

We raced through the tax forms at the back of a big church. There wasn't a crack in it. It was a temple to cement with lines of small chairs under a high roof that was grey and plain. There was no stained glass, the windows were like elephants' eyes, too small for the frame cut in dull order. They left you gasping for light, it was the colour of a dark day. Clergy taxation services are a rare bunch – we were seen with precision. We waded through the figures. I had spent hours on the floor of the shed adding up receipts for biscuits and books – you have to keep them all. What a job, though, trawling round the country, going through vicars' finances. I wonder how honest we are. There's the odd tale – the baptism collection going missing, and there was one bloke who hyped the figures for marriages and funerals. These are all set by the church commissioners, a marriage service is currently £127. The vicar in question was charging it out at £450 and pocketing the difference. Another one took to robbing building societies in the West-Country villages. He didn't reckon on closed-circuit television and the power of his public face. One of the fine things is that we are not paid a great deal. It does actually matter in the sense that we put our money where our mouth is. I don't mind it for myself; the mountainous difficulties arise when families are involved. In that sense being a Catholic priest has its luxuries.

The Prime Minister wants to alter the appointments process. There is apparently a Mr Holroyd who presents Parliament with the names of those who are to be considered for tomorrow's bishops. These names have just 'emerged' – emerged from where? The Bishop of Woolwich is calling for disestablishment. Let's hope it comes sooner rather than later – our relationship to the crown and the state is in danger of becoming a fatal distraction. We are expected to play poodle, and by and large the church has obliged. We are rolled out on state occasions wearing our aunt's curtains on our back.

I bought the pattern when I came here – they wanted family services, someone to pep things up a bit. It was all wrong. Like a baby I obliged, thinking this was the way forward, this was the model to work from to attract new blood into old veins. The curacy was the same, we just needed a few modern pills and everything would be all right. No, we just need God, to know our need of God; it's no good starting from anywhere else except there. It is the alpha and the omega; what happens between those two points is infinitely variable according to the culture and era, but it is our relationship with God that is critical, not our relationship with the State, the Council, the Crown. It's not why priests become priests, it's not why people bravely come on Sundays – it's a lead weight, we should cut the chain.

The *Sunday Times* magazine was open on the table. On the right-hand page was a picture of a human ribcage – the victim had been burned and then buried. The mulch in the middle must have been what was left of his internal organs after the fire and earth had opened it up, these unmistakable properties. On the left-hand page was a £28,000 car; the driver had just come out of make-up. Both images were from the same continent. There was nothing between them, silver-plated savagery at its shiniest. We're in fashionable denial about war; it's clearly potentially very exciting to gamble with death, must set your synapses on fire. It's not for everyone – we're not all born soldiers – but there are undoubtedly some people that are good at it. No wonder they don't talk about it. The shock of coming home for some of them after the Second World War, the ordinariness of it, must have been desperately hard to come to terms with, to have done things that on a normal day you would have been hanged for, to sit on sofas in painted rooms holding tea cups having bayoneted other young men to death must have created an awful inner loneliness. I've buried killers. Their wives, their children, all say the same thing: he never talked about it. The opening twenty minutes of *Saving Private Ryan* is an extraordinary piece of film direction, the way Steven Spielberg achieves the silences, there in the midst of all that total bloody mayhem, the way he takes you through Tom Hanks to the point where you are lost. It is the silence beyond the guns that's so awful.

Have we given up on Isaiah's dream of turning swords into ploughshares, guns into goalposts, tanks into tables? Along with chewing gum, televisions and computers the twentieth century will always leave its war memorials, scratched in stained glass, ordinary names banged into stone, guns left under angels. The blood of those is in all our veins. I have lived forty-one years and it's there, all day in the scenery, sometimes it hits you full in the face, D-Day, Omaha Beach, the Somme, Spitfires, the Enigma Code, Hiroshima, the Bay of Pigs, Suez, Vietnam. I have ingested all of them; it is compulsory poison. We call this peacetime and yet doodle bugs and shrapnel rain down on us every day. Have you ever seen the shadows of jets as they fly over the land? It is as if we are caught in the spaces between them, as if they made an invisible net that holds all of us in it. The blitz goes on, rockets and bombs, mortars, gas, ethnic cleansing, massacres, dead hands reaching out through the soil. You know they could have been yours. No, we're still at war, still in war. Peace has been defined by war; as long as we are not fighting we are at peace, we live in peacetime, or so the theory goes. This yardstick we use is no measure of peace, not if we can pick it up and use it as a sword as well. The sickness of violence haunts just about every middle-sized English town. These are unpleasant places on Friday and Saturday nights, they are not safe. Casualty departments in hospitals pick up the pieces, clean up the blood, stitch the lips, but there are more bruises than that, and yet this is known as peacetime. We live in fear – the level of fear we endure as individuals is terrible. The level of fear many elderly people endure is even worse. We are all of us ashamed by it, because we simply put up with it as best we can.

Evil always manifests itself in oppression; it is anti-life in every way, its aim is the death of the soul, it enslaves. It's fashionable perhaps to ignore it, to satisfy ourselves that as children of the Enlightenment, as we have eloquently called it, we are almost untouched by its blunt excess. But we carry it, it makes our excuses and forgives us with a wave of a hand and we become hypnotised by its easy manner and are happy to believe in a fabulous lack of consequences and there goes hell with all its quaint torn tongues and cold flames. The logic is that we can now quite easily ignore the limits of the medieval imagination; it has become a museum, like Alcatraz. As long as we see hell in that fashion we will become increasingly unaware at some point of the existence of evil, that we have paid for progress with our souls. We have indulged ourselves in the ludicrous thinking that poison doesn't taste so sweet, like champagne.

My generation grew up being told not to forget war, not to forget those who had given their lives. We celebrated heroes we could never have been, we endured the shadows in concentration camps, the mud of the trenches, the dogfights that happened above us before we were born. Last week on television we were shown some rare footage of a field full of young dead German men. We were told this was retribution, a partisan killing, part of what went on at the Russian front. Most of them had ears missing, eyes gauged out, their testicles had been cut off. It's as if we are being primed in case we are needed to behave in the same way. We have not forgotten we are still at war. We have, though, forgotten peace in the process: true, true peace. Maybe we have forgotten how to believe in it. But Isaiah's dream still stands – it is not impossible at all. Imagine streets that were safe to walk in, a country that prided itself on peace, real peace. How many times have you seen that bomb go off at Hiroshima, how many times have you seen an atom bomb exploding on the screen? The weight of that image is awful, awful; it haunts all of us, imprinted on our souls, that for all our art, our grace, our ingenuity, that is what we have become, that is what we are all capable of. Yes, it's true and we need to know it, but we are also capable of standing in front of the tank in Tianamen Square. Yes, the Cold War froze all of us in the West. I'm not sure we have stopped shivering yet, but we must. It's time we moved on. Peace, peace.

I walked past Ridley Hall last night. There was a party in the garden opposite. I peered over the wooden fence. There was a lot of blue satin and 'The Girl from Ipanema' was spilling through the trees. Chinese lanterns hung on the branches. It is an exquisite garden, a great place for a party. I used to go there after lunch with a head full of thumping theology and watch the squirrels spitting at each other and the spring crocuses falling over themselves.

There was a Deanery Synod meeting tonight. It was meant to be in Caldecote Village Hall but it was locked. I finally clocked the A4 sheet covered in thin biro redirecting everyone to Bourn Church. Most of the meeting was classic comedy, the clergy retiring to the back of the church to elect a secretary who wasn't there, and a new member of the standing committee – the only one who didn't look at the ceiling when it was suggested. The laity were left at the front to elect a vice chairperson. Most of them are new; this was their first adventure into the bowels of the Church of England. About halfway through the meeting I turned round to see a new curate clearly praying that items 8, 9 and 10 would spontaneously evaporate from view. We then all got bounced into voting for funding the board of social responsibility, which was completely farcical, because after a brief debate no one was any the wiser as to what it actually does. But it was a very good day. The social service advisor in the Diocesan Office was fantastic, she made one phone call which really made a great deal of difference to a family that are in desperate need. Our prayer this morning found something, was a part of something far greater than we can know, God in the spaces between us. You do visit another world in prayer. You become part of something so much bigger than yourself. It is really an awareness of the being of God; that being is surely with us all the time. In prayer, through prayer, you become aware of the joins – the saints take it way beyond the seams.

Rather strangely, humble pie usually tastes sweet. I was up before the Barton Parish Council apologising for the embarrassment of the press release that I should not have released when I did; it inspired well over 300 phone calls about the Arbory Trust. Village halls are wonderful buildings, the dust left by weddings and wakes and discos. They are locked in their time: never quite clean, the chairs are uncomfortable, the tables are cheap, everything gets scratched.

They were very generous actually. I was keen that they should judge the proposal on its merits and not be jaundiced by the rash actions of an over-eager enthusiast. It's truly summer now, the still trees ripen in the sun, have a perfect sense of childhood about them; they seem the way they always were. Newton Church is wonderful. There's a wedding there tomorrow; the vicar who was my pastoral tutor left in March to become Canon of Bury Cathedral. His parting gift was this wedding. There was at some point a school in Newton that taught metalwork – in the church there is the most incredible art nouveau copper cross. The memorial to those who died in the First and Second World Wars is in the same style; garnished in ivy, it is almost pink. It's quite extraordinary. As well there is possibly one of the most exquisite angels in marble I have ever seen, higher on the wall, half in the light, half out. There is a simple unassuming beauty about the place. We have almost surrendered this as important; it's not about marble and copper, glass and stones, it's what inspired them that matters. Someone said today that the Hindus had got it right, they had a religion that blended into the strands of everyday life. They're right. Christianity has been removed from our humanity by becoming a moral code which has in turn become more important than the faith that inspired it. We sell ourselves on sin, God becomes this get-out-of-jail card, but we are made beautiful by beauty. It is not giving up sin that makes us beautiful, it is what we replace sin with, it is recognising our own beauty.

The notion that we *can* give up sin is ludicrous; it is customarily partnered with the even more ludicrous proposition that Christians are somehow less sinful than pagans. Apart from being quite untrue – Christians are riddled with sin – having taken on the notion that God is real, that Christ is certain, that the Holy Spirit, the living breathing being that is God is alive, to accept all that in fact raises the viscosity of our sin. To look upon the world and declare it sinful, to judge it by its failings disregards Christian history and essential frailty, the weakness in all of us that underlines our human being. How many times have we seen closed sects offering salvation? The price of course is that you sign up, you sell your soul; it's an old trick, demonise 'them' to make 'us' feel better. This has nothing to do with serving humanity; it is self-serving right the way down the line. In that sense the gap between church and society widens all the time. To impose Christian morals on others is disgraceful; by all means choose them for yourself, but to play the pious card, to ice piety with power, disregards and contradicts love completely.

The wedding was wonderful: hats, sunshine, singing. I always struggle to keep back the tears when the vows are being said. I then raced back, mowed the lawn, hurried supper and shot off to Harlton where there was a concert to raise money to send a student to Africa. All those playing had just finished school – clean clear faces. The church was full to the brim. Summer's in full flow; it was hot today, even the flies got lazy.

Gordon doesn't look well. He is very pale, almost as white as his linen jacket. He's one of the most generous men I know, his life outlined by a rich Christianity. He carves his sermons out of the Bible and has the enthusiasm of a child when he talks about the church filling with young people. I was so glad he was there tonight in Harlton to see it; he arrived looking too thin. These young people are far more sussed than I ever was. They have an integrity and a presence beyond the reach of most of the priests I know. In many ways my job is perhaps to prepare the church for them. To make sure they have space and a creative environment, to enable them to be far more relaxed than my own generation are, to create an environment where they can be priests, not administrators, liturgy experts, faculty bearers, C of E officers, board of social responsibility, overseers. The public don't want Evangelicals, Catholics, Liberals, Charismatics; they want priests. They want an end to all this whingeing that's going on. This is an amazing job, if you can tolerate the institution that comes with it, if you can hang on to God because of it really and not believe the compliments you receive, understand that you are called to the edges, not to some ridiculous throne, that what you have been given is far greater than you could ever repay, and still not stop trying. They want priests, ministers, they want people who have given up the world for them, to bear their pain and terror, to lead them in right pathways and guide their feet in the ways of peace, to spread a table before them, to anoint their head with oil, to lead them beside still waters, to walk with them through the valley of the shadow of death, to wash their feet. They want to know, as Jeremy Begbie said, that God delights in us. He preached in Harlton on Sunday, he was my doctrine lecturer from theological college. He was then and is now nothing other than inspirational.

Amazing: the concert in Harlton on Sunday was to raise money to send this young man to Africa to work for Cross Links; he needed £1,304.16. When everything was counted up that is exactly the sum that was there; not a penny more, not a penny less.

It's Saturday. It started at about 8.30 with four messages on the answerphone, on to Harlton at 9.15 to inter some ashes at 9.30. Something was worrying the geese on the other side of the churchyard. They ran their mad voices through Psalm 91 and hissed as the casket was lowered into the earth. The glebe land was beginning to change colour as the rows of folding tables and white canvas marquees filled with voices and shadows. The art exhibition in the church was already up, paintings of the lakes, pots of pastel flowers, zebras on silk, black and white photographs of frost, traction engines with wet wheels, the vicar in a crumpled hat, the painters torching his vanity. A squirrel had trashed my study – the door had been open all night. There are squirrel droppings everywhere: in the fax machine, on the desk, a perfect pawprint on the undertaker's cheque. I raided the garden for vegetables, today was the moment of truth: three courgettes, four potatoes, three carrots, two lettuces, four onions. There was a brief meeting at eleven o'clock.

I picked up some money on the way back to Harlton – I begged £600. It wasn't hard, two phone calls; it's for the family who lost their mother three weeks ago. The two older daughters are going it alone rather than split the family up, they're all deciding to stay together. One daughter's working to support the younger sons. To fill the gap between income support and the rent bill they needed one month's rent to keep them going. I ran back to Harlton with the vegetables then drove to give the family the money, stopped at the pub for a coke and a bite to eat, drove back to Harlton and opened the fête. I had this portable PA system which howls with feedback when the wind blows against the microphone. My wife said I looked like some dodgy journalist at a race meeting. I think the balloon race just about covered the cost of the hydrogen cylinder – two of the yellow balloons escaped from the lattice and were caught in the trees before we let them all go.

I spent the afternoon having the most extraordinary collection of short conversations. I was dragged by the ears between pig breeding, education, politics, church architecture, football, heart attacks, birth, the falling butterfly count, hymn number 472, wireworm, prayer, basketball, pollution, and of course the millennium. I was put in the stocks, covered in cream, had a bucket put on my head, cold water poured down the back of my trousers, our eldest son fell off the bouncy castle, our youngest daughter went into complete apoplexy when the balloons were let loose. The potatoes came first, the onions and the lettuce managed a second apiece, the carrots and the courgettes bombed.

Have you ever thought what 'being saved' actually means? It's a divisive set of words actually; it assumes you either are or you aren't, which I suppose is exactly what it is meant to imply. There were these Charismatics on television last night claiming God was turning fillings into gold. The Dean of St Paul's was sceptical: with Rwanda, Northern Ireland and the wastelands of the world, why would God start turning amalgam into gold? The Charismatics essentially need something charismatic; there were all these awful shots of the cameras zooming in on people's molars while they were trying to smile.

Christianity surely isn't about 'being saved'; essentially, it is understanding that you are loved, that you are extraordinary, that you are holy, a sacrament of God. That knowledge in itself saves you, redeems you, holds you, fuels your being with the being of God. Speaking in tongues surely does not separate you from humanity – it joins you to the root of your humanity and in so doing to all humanity. You do not join a club, you are joined to all. It is not a gift given to be used as holy currency; it is there to be spent on all. We say when we find these gifts within us that they are the making of us, and in many ways they are: the sinner sins, the jugglers juggle, the doctor heals, politicians inspire. David Bellamy said that he knew every single grass, its name, its feel, its colour; he said it was just something that he could do. Maybe Capability Brown could just do landscapes; Martin Luther King could just speak through the mire of bigotry; Stephen Hawkins just travel the infinite forces of physics. These have been gifts that have touched all of us, the point where you are taken beyond yourself, the point where your being is. Bjorn Borg's heartbeat used to go down, apparently, when he was playing competitive tennis. Why then have we locked up this thing called holiness, enshrined it, put it in a kitsch castle, embalmed it in ridiculous words, separated it from normality, put it apart from life? It *is* life, all life.

July . . . .

We struggled on Sunday really – there were fifteen of us in Great Eversden. I am failing there, no other description will do; the PCC was pretty torrid on Thursday. I was whipped for failing to mention that the New Testaments that had been bought for all the churches were to be paid for by all the churches. I thought I'd jumped through that hoop, I hadn't. I'm not very good at doing things in triplicate and was made to sit on that point for about fifteen minutes. The guilt is awful – it covers everything in grease, sticks in your eyes and then on your fingers. The *Church Times* was comparing the Church of England to animals on the front page. Apparently in the research commissioned by the archbishop's council we came out as elephants. No great surprises on that one. The only way round this is to spend much more time there. I wish I could.

This is really the fruits of one parish having its own way for fifteen years. The whole thing has become self-defining; they opted out because they wanted to do things their own way, and here's the proof as to why they should continue: a vicar they see once a month and for funerals and weddings. I don't blame them for feeling sore about it; it's not a ministry, it's a function, that's my fault. The trouble is that with more than two churches ministry becomes a function – the practical side of running things engulfs the spiritual purpose of existence completely. Rural ministry continues to be eroded at an alarming rate because of this. You can only attend to the urgent. Christ seemed to balance the urgent with the incidental. The best news was that a charismatic house church had taken to using the village hall every Sunday morning. I was told this with alarm. What the whole situation needs is quality time that I don't have. It is hard enough to run one church properly, let alone four, which is a recipe for failure; there must be a way through this, however, there simply must be.

To compound what was a pretty awful evening, a complaint has been made through a third party that I asked a bereaved couple for two hundred quid up front before I would consider taking the funeral. The complaint comes from a friend of the bereaved who phoned a priest she knew up north, who quite understandably phoned the archdeacon straight away, who then called the rural dean, who then called me. The trouble is that you can't really refute this successfully, not really. There is always going to be an element of doubt that remains; it's very, very serious. While I have never, and would never dream of doing anything like that, the whole thing will remain unproved one way or the other. The archdeacon was quite brilliant; he simply said he couldn't believe it. I have spoken to the person who apparently made these accusations and will be seeing her tomorrow. She denies having said any of it. Mud tastes awful. You are vulnerable as a priest because in many situations you are dealing with people at their most vulnerable. What is seen through tears is quite a different world. Probably the worst thing you could say is that the church takes advantage of the situation, making mileage out of tragedy, turning babies holy, sacred, when that is clearly what their parents feel about them anyway, drinking the dew in lovers' eyes, turning up whenever there's champagne or tea and cakes on offer and arrogantly explaining everything. Yes, that is nothing other than conceit; it's awful, but because it's so awful we're probably over-sensitive to it, and that is the last thing that most of us would want to do.

Well, it all seems to have sorted itself out. The confusion seems to have arisen over the fees. Apart from marriages I don't usually discuss fees. But in this particular instance I was asked how much the service would cost and it added up, with the organist, to around two hundred pounds. The family came to the church with that money in cash. They were not aware that the undertaker's bill includes all of that and that the undertaker always pays the minister before the service. Anyway, they were brilliant about it. Wires do get crossed. We go to Devon tomorrow.

The sea is silver. Mouth Mill is as close as you can get to paradise. It's a grey cottage built from the stones on the beach. It sits one hundred yards up from the sea and there are steep wooded slopes on either side, a stream fifty feet from the door. You are caught in this bowl of green oaks, ash, sycamore; there are slow worms under the stones. The beach is all boulders and pebbles, pink, grey, green, gothic cliffs swarming with gulls. When the Atlantic is roaring you can hear it in the house, the wind blasts up the valley. We used to come in winter, lock ourselves into the one room with a fire. There's no electricity – there's a gas stove and three gas lights. Upstairs it's candles. If there was a heavy snowfall you would have to eat the mussels which cover the rocks at low tide. The pages in the books which are everywhere are yellow, the handles wobble on the pans, the immersion is fickle, one flame that either does or doesn't light. The wood burner cranks the one radiator and heats a tank wrapped in shot blankets to a bearable temperature in the bathroom, which is an afterthought, tacked on to the side, full of cobwebs and cracked paint. The butterflies travel in gangs: Silver-washed Fritillaries, Commas, Red Admirals, Painted Ladies, Skippers, busy in the neck-high grass. You can only reach the house by the one track that winds and bumps through a huge wood. The colours change with the light. Today the sunshine has been unbroken. We left Haslingfield at four and arrived here at half past eleven.

The most disturbing aspect of it all is that it is almost home; it has been the one constant place while we were sent swinging through college and a curacy. This has been the only place that is apart from it all and yet part of it all. It is the one house that is common not only to the past but to all of it. There is a bat now looping across what's left of the light. I suppose I have a handful of things left, momentoes of a former life, here and there. There is the odd panther parlour in London but really everything other than the relationships has gone, been painted over. It's right you should give it all, not as much as you can but, as Christ said, if you want to go the whole way you must give up everything.

This morning a mist came in, you could see each drop. The sea was quiet too, solemn, stuck to the cliffs. Once we drove up and reached higher Clovelly we were out of its grip. We had lunch at the Smithy Inn in Welcombe then cut down to the beach on a one-car road – sunshine splashing off the windscreen, bracken and brambles scratching the paint on the car. The children spent the afternoon screaming at the waves that were falling off the Atlantic. The yellow wagtails have a nest in the old mill. I imagine living here sometimes but you would either end up wise or mad. Is there anything in between? What are you?

The waves this afternoon at Welcombe were almost perfect. They would come in patches – you could follow the big ones in from about 400 metres out. They travelled in packs, then came and thundered on the shore. It was very hot – the children couldn't really stand on the stones – but there was this big swell and an offshore wind that would whip up the crest at that extraordinary point just before they fell. The beach at Welcombe is lined with rock channels that lead directly into the sea. At the end there is sand. When the tide comes in the water is funnelled up these channels; it comes raining down. We made some walls but they fell. It's been blissful, blue all week. It's getting hotter. A farmer was spinning for sea bass on the beach this evening. About three years ago this huge shoal of mackerel came in. I stood on the rocks with India and we watched as the gannets bombed the water. In Clovelly they were hauling them in on rods from the beach. He said that it used to happen every year, the sea bass would come in behind the mackerel. He also said that he'd met a businessman who had paid an inordinate amount of money for one day's shooting; they were sitting up against the wall and he said to him, How lucky you are to live here. We go home tonight.

We came back along the A303. It has to be the route 66 of England. Kula Shaker have enshrined it. I'd like to know how old it is – it is a rollercoaster of immense proportions gliding through Wiltshire. The roads were jammed up; it became quieter at about midnight. Going into the West Country was pretty much bumper to bumper, to catch the eclipse perhaps. Sarah is going to Newquay, to the same hotel where she was on honeymoon. We had a healing service in Haslingfield this morning. I spent most of it grappling with tears. Everyone came up to the altar for the laying on of hands. It was beautiful, the sun pouring in through the south windows raising the dust.

There were sixty-seven emails when I turned the computer on. One of them ranted that we shouldn't have the agenda of the church set by the world. I agree – I used not to. I always thought we should be there on the bus heading off with every whim set by what is clever PR. No, no more. Our agenda is already set – the temptations not to follow it, not to ultimately follow Christ, are immense and we have perhaps been caught up in a willingness to please as our loss of identity prevailed. The Church of England cannot be exemplified, justified by fêtes, brick, chairs, choirs and carpets. That is not what it's about and we will never convince anybody otherwise by PR and advertising. Advertising and PR can be effective but not in the conventional sense. Nothing can actually be better than following the words of Christ rather than indulging ourselves in endless missions; surely that is what we must concentrate on, being and breathing with God. The danger is always that the wonder, the simplicity of that, the purity, is actually compromised by our worldliness. Why on earth should we need to be worldly? We are in essence other-worldly, based on the impossible, drinking the unprovable, giving away gold, walking on water. Christ spoke to the inner person, the real untamed lunatic in all of us. He cut straight to the essence of our being. The world is oiled by the outer, not by the inner. The outer is easier to manipulate; it is the actor, the actress, that we presume we all have to be. It deals with survival not being. Christ speaks to our being, our eternity; he had no truck with the outer, with pretence, with appearances: the appearance of power, the appearance of position, the appearance of virtue, the appearance of worthlessness. It didn't matter.

Well, we finally have arrived at a way forward in Haslingfield as far as the fabric goes. We'll be doing a bit of work inside and outside and put a ready-made hut on a small piece of glebe land that's overrun with damsons. Rumour has it that it is the plague pit down there; I've been told that several times in long low tones. There are definitely some broken gravestones at the dip in the glebe, couched in ivy, buried under moss. When we moved here there was a muntjac deer in the garden; it would walk in between the brambles at the back and the damsons of the glebe. Three tawny owl chicks have recently been fledged from their nest. It must have been in one of the trees at the back of the garden; they call all night incessantly. I watched one of the parents hand over a limp mouse which was swallowed head first in about fifteen seconds. This morning there was a green woodpecker on the road that leads to the village green.

I've been able to do some visiting. Other people's houses always seem quieter than this one; the phone doesn't interrupt everything. I love houses where people have lived for a long time, forty or fifty years. They have a sense of stillness about them. I spoke to a man yesterday who drove one of the landing craft up on to the Normandy beaches on D-Day. He said thirty of the soldiers were dead before he reached the beach. He brought as many bodies back as he could before doing the trip again. He said we lost 10,000 on the first day.

This morning we had a communion service. On Monday I was asked to cover for the priest on the other side of the hill; he's organised this service once a month in the pub. We sat there with ashtrays on the table, the coffee machine speaking in tongues, what was wonderful was that the landlord made very few allowances for the fact that we were there at all – he didn't whisper ordering the food for the evening on the phone in the middle of the Eucharistic prayer. He very kindly cut up some cake for us at the end and suggested we all have our harvest lunch there in September. We can pray anywhere we like. Too many people think God is there on the other side of the stained glass – God is only there because they are there. We are not loved any more or any less in church than we are at home or at work. We have been fooled into believing that we are. We may reconcile ourselves to the fact that we are loved when we are sitting in the hard pews, but the revelation comes with choosing over time to be in the presence of God. The discipline is a fine thing, but we have confused the place with the purpose. The purpose is in fact placeless, timeless even; surely every second is a miracle in itself.

It was hot up until this morning. Now it is completely still; everything utterly motionless apart from the birds. The sky is a constant numinous grey, heavy with water, the leaves lowered, shining with it. The fields on the way to the Queen's Head in Newton have round bales all over them; the unharvested areas – the colour of sand – stretch right to the horizon. Tractors with trailers full of grain hack through the villages in fifth gear. There is grain spilled on every corner – it's all over the road, too much for the birds, brushed up against the kerb in long golden lines. Imagine in Old Testament times, widows, orphans and foreigners were allowed to glean the fields, to pick up grain from the ground that the harvesters had missed. It must have been precious. Our biological survival has been almost superseded by our material survival. Life itself has become perhaps more certain. In the West, at any rate, our scientists are intent on dissecting the universe, to prove and thus to improve. That's the theory. But what are we here to discover, what have we come to look for: that we need oxygen to breathe, that chocolate is good for us, that there is life on Mars? What have we made of that process of discovery, what has it become? A scramble for material security, superior knowledge, another awful victory over chaos? What sort of dominion do we exercise and, more importantly, do we perceive?

It is a perception perhaps that has been frozen in favour of proof, our souls becalmed, lost in a sea of reason. Is the universe no more than reasonable, the rainforest reasonable, love reasonable, the waves reasonable? Is that what it has become: grass reduced to pig meat, pigs to bacon? Are the cathedrals reasonable buildings, the old Ethiopians on television last night dressed in yellow, their church hewn from volcanic rock dug downwards, living in rooms no bigger than this desk, waiting for death and paradise, is that a reasonable act? Can you reason with the rain, reason with your soul, can you reason with the chaos of love? I can't. The church is out of touch, they will say, out of touch with what? Reason, probably. Old men muttering in psalms, praying for grace and forgiveness; thank God for that, thank God for them.

At theological college I can remember this passion to make God relevant. We dressed him, her, up in the coolest clothes we could find, trying to impose credibility – our version, whatever it was, Evangelical, Catholic, Charismatic, Liberal – but we'd already fallen into the trap, we'd bought the labels. They are no different really from Nike, Reebok; they are different competing brands, that's all. We came out wearing them, all of us. We were so busy standing up for the truth that we'd completely missed the fact that we'd signed everything over to become badly paid civil servants. We were schooled in the doctrines of the institution, the mannerisms of the institution, the songs of the institution, the theology of the institution. God came through the cracks, kicked us when she could, he could; we were not schooled in stillness, in contemplation, in the ways of evil, in the multi-resonant voice of God; we were not schooled in wonder, in the healing, in the moment, in being. Maybe I wasn't listening. We should be Jedi but we were being turned into Jeeves. The old Bishop of Huntingdon was the closest to Yoda I have ever met. Our curacies are taken up with learning the ropes up, down, along, cross, sign here, dot this. I was lucky my master was threaded in the Fen sky. As priests we are bounced from one committee to another. I'm going to resign from all of them. I think I have no right to chair the PCC, no right at all. I would rather take four assemblies a week than sit on the board of governors really. The outreach committee does not need the Methodist minister or myself – we need to re-focus on God. If we had a job description it should read 'Love your neighbour as yourself.' It must take years to master that, surely.

A rather strange e-mail arrived this morning. It was entitled 'Old Jewish proverb: He who thinketh that he standeth take heed lest he fall.' My ego is a ruddy great ball and chain that clatters. 'Old shortarse proverb: He who doth not stand very tall is not so worried about the fall.'

August

It has rained for two days and everything is damp. The eclipse is tomorrow, millions of people looking up into fog. I always find that time in prayer when the words stop, when we have said whatever we thought was important, more beautiful than the words themselves. The silence afterwards often says more to us, there is more in it than all the words that went before when we have grown accustomed to the stillness, when we have emptied ourselves of ourselves and recognised the infinite space beyond our concerns.

The eclipse lacquered everything. The sun was clearly visible; we stood there with our cardboard glasses looking at this orange crescent in various stages of decline. It didn't go dark here at all, it was more a numinous half-light. The ultraviolet was removed from everything, the rooks kept on arguing and the shadows struggled but the quality of light on the ground, the way in which it thinned almost before you was rare, rare indeed. Maybe it was just because we were looking.

I have told the standing committee that I wish to resign from all our PCC meetings, and as many other functional things as possible, in the hope of making something more pastoral, something less like a civil servant and more like a servant.

They seemed quite enthusiastic, they seemed to agree that being bound by the purely practical was self-defeating. You can of course be immersed in it and not be bound by it, but I have not yet met anyone who has managed it; those who are judged successful by the standards of institutions are the ones who have been most successfully institutionalised, perhaps. Some people survive it but most of us don't; my only concern is that it's 'makeup'. It's easy in the summer with the evening sewing purples and blues on the fields, the air smelling of wheat, to dream dreams; the winter, however, will test them. I aim to walk, to walk as much as possible, to put away the car, to spend as much time as possible with the people of these parishes, not on the committees that represent them. I aim to pray on the paths between the villages. Is that strategy? Or is that ministry? From the outside, the church looks very similar to a large City corporation, a bank, an insurance company, we use the same typefaces. Maybe that is what we feel respectable success should be. I don't think Jesus Christ was respectable; respected, yes, but this craving for respectability, this need to be approved of, has weakened us tremendously, thankfully.

It's very quiet in the villages; you really do get the sense that most of the people are away. It's a very gentle time, a thinking time, the pressure is off and you can wallow in summer shadows. Why go away and take the noise with you? We have found an administrator for the Arbory Trust. We interviewed two people in this colourless room at the diocesan office – it had every shade of grey in it. It is one of the most sombre buildings I have ever been into, the combination of sixty-watt light bulbs, magnolia paint and endless carpet squares makes you feel you've arrived in that awful house at the end of *Silence of the Lambs* – what a revolting film that was. Anita got the job. So it's off and running, trees instead of gravestones; should be good for the woodpeckers. The leader of the Savoy Jazz Band called and we've arranged a concert in Haslingfield Church for mid-September, he's flying over a hot clarinettist from Sweden. Does God dance? Absolutely. There are leaves in the road, I picked up the car this morning: £835. I managed to knacker the sump, the radiator and the suspension all in one hit as I went over rather a large bump. It's Harris's birthday, he managed to open nine presents just about simultaneously. We now share the house with R2D2 and a Naboo fighter, which is an exquisite yellow design. It's fork-shaped, a hybrid of a stealth bomber and a wasp, covered in comic-book colours.

The Diocesan Office is the mother ship, here we have the youth officer, the covenant secretary and the diocesan secretary. You get the feeling the entertainment budget runs dry after you've bought a loaf of Mother's Pride and three tomatoes. Then there's the surveyor's office that runs all the vicarages; whenever you phone up there's always a crisis, oil tanks constructed with tin from an indefinable source have spontaneously combusted. When we moved into the vicarage the horse-trading was wonderful: the choice of carpets was between two. The diocesan surveyor had also managed to pick up some kitchen units which, he informed me, were knocked down to half price in the sale where everything had already been knocked down to half price; he then negotiated a thirty per cent discount on that. I think he must have bought the whole lot for the cost of the handles. But it's a fair system, bishops get the same carpets as we do. The trouble is the whole thing is set against the law of diminishing returns. I reckon it's set to hit meltdown in about 2004 which is when all the central heating systems, the bathroom taps, the obscure make of sanitation systems are set to buckle in unison as the result of everything that's been done on the cheap over the last forty years. It is as if you could be caught in an endless loop of ''Twas on a Monday morning when the gas man came to call, the gas tap wouldn't turn, I wasn't getting gas at all, he pulled out all the skirting boards to try to find the main and I had to get the carpenter to put them back again.' My wife's revenge has been acid pink walls, multi-coloured banisters and a bathroom inspired by the colours of tutti-fruttis.

It's money again, I'm afraid. The church doesn't have enough to cope with the demands made upon it. We have to sort this out; living off the bottom of the barrel is fine but we have to reorganise, redefine our priorities. We can't keep going with the system that has this etiquette and process earthed in the eighteenth century. It has not evolved and that fact is in part responsible for crumbling walls and riddled confidence. We need to charge a great deal more for the services we do perform. Over the mix-up in the funeral fees the undertakers sent me a copy of their bill; they in fact charge the service out at £120, the regulation church fee which is split between the local church and the diocese is £58, so in that respect the undertaker is making more out of the service than we are. The wedding couples that come in are always gobsmacked at how cheap the marriage service is. I always try to see couples three times, then there's the rehearsal and the service itself. The fee for all of that is £127; it's cheaper than hiring the car to chauffeur the bride and groom, it's cheaper than a photographer, it's cheaper than the dress, it's cheaper than the cake. Baptisms cost nothing at all. We should be charging a great deal more for what we do: £500 for a wedding in church, £300 for a funeral service, £200 for a burial, £50 for a baptism. If people can't afford it, and there will be some that can't, then the vicar must have the jurisdiction, having cleared it from above, to reduce the fees. There have been times when we've charged nothing at all here, that's fine. But we have to start charging non-charitable rates for what we do. If people want a proper service from the church then they will have to start paying properly for it.

Sarah is back from Torquay. She said it was very cloudy on the morning of the eclipse and that it was very moving. After our prayers this morning we talked about the idea of stepping aside from the PCCs. Both she and the other churchwardens in the Eversdens think it's a good idea. We'll aim to have a trial year next year, I think. The Archbishop of Canterbury is on record as saying that what he calls the trivia of parish life – which he defines as getting caught up in parish politics, the flower rota – is getting in the way of spirituality. He goes on to say that too many mediocre clergy are caught up in 'churchy affairs'. I agree, but he cannot essentially abdicate from a system that he is responsible for, lay it at the feet of the clergy and blame them for the state we are all in. This state we are all in is, in part at least, down to the ridiculous and cumbersome management models that exist to prop up the so-called authority of the clergy, the form filling that goes on to change a light fitting, to plant a yew tree; the fact that there are books written about PCC management is testament to a system that has lost its way down its own corridors. It has meant that the church has been held to ransom by those with the stamina for the small print and a penchant for petty politics. We have consequently expended far too much energy on putting out fires rather than starting them. The Archbishop of Canterbury is surely right to be concerned, but if the object is really to free us all from the chains of 'churchianity' then he could start by cutting as many of them as possible.

There was a time up in the Fens when we had a fog for eight days in a row; it seeped into your ears, crept down your throat. By the seventh day everyone had adjusted to it, people appeared to slow down, they wrapped up their faces. I remember this swan that had become completely disorientated standing in the road opposite the church. I tried to corral it through the big iron gates into the graveyard but it ran off down the road, opened its wings and was gone.

The air has cooled; it's singed with autumn. The blackberries and elderberries are full of rain, their skins shine, the ends of the brambles and the elder hang heavy with their weight. It is a miracle really that from molten rock and ash we end up with life. It is the fruit of love. Are our fourscore years and ten as incidental as the lichen on the roofs, the wood pigeons clapping their wings in June, a fly caught in a bottle? The Evangelicals constantly try to persuade us of our own importance. We are jewels in God's eyes, that I do not doubt, but it makes us princes of nothing other than our own imaginations.

The love of God which comes through the cracks of our brokenness in prayer carries no weight actually, no punishing gifts of guilt. However foul, however tepid, timid, cowardly, whatever the perceived awfulness of the sins that are regularly committed by my own weak soul, the response has always been one of love. It might have been C.S. Lewis who said, 'we are loved into heaven' – it may all sound rather flattering. But there is surely no point in hatred, I'm not sure God can hate. This doesn't mean you end up with some well-meaning old man; I think to love in the face of hatred must be the hardest thing we are asked to do, to overcome hatred, to absorb it and to love. Stephen Sykes said that probably the most important quality for a priest was humility: to retain humility through all the siren flattery, the blunt authority, the rank derision that comes your way. If after thirty-five years you could achieve some of that, that indeed would be worth the sum of every second. Basil Hume had it, had some of it. I don't believe it comes from anything other than dependence on God and looking to God. We live in a society obsessed by strength, by power – who wields it and how. The church has become tangled up in all of it, too tangled, we have no rights to it at all. We actually have no need of it either. We are surely charged to liberate, to try to describe the view. I'm not sure that we have any automatic rights at all to be debating the cost of living in the House of Lords.

The clutch has gone on the car. Moving the gearstick has become like forcing a crowbar through broken concrete pieces. I don't feel I can ask for the money, I took so much flak last time. I didn't mention the £823 for the radiator, the sump and suspension. I didn't feel that it was fair under the circumstances to ask for the money after I had taken it off across the fields, drawn by the intoxicating scent of meadows and the sea. It was the point where everything met an end and a beginning.

The Parish Council turned down the idea of the Portacabins at the back of the graveyard; these were for the Sunday club and the Sunday school. It went to the county council and they've canned it as well. The building work starts in October so they'll be out of the room for the Sunday club, not that the tower rooms in Haslingfield are designed for that sort of thing; in winter all that's missing are penguins and arctic foxes. I did volunteer to put a Portacabin in the garden but I've gone off that idea. No, they will have to use our house. I'll have to talk to Jacs.

Tomorrow it's Little Eversden, the church which backs onto a farmyard, the metal silos set in concrete, the gleaming modern barns in with some tumbling cart sheds where the thin nettles grasp at the light. It's a very quiet place; there are all the ingredients there for a religious community perhaps. There was this thought to begin something, a place where young people could come and chill out, come and experience what a morning's silence means, come to a place free from labels and peer pressure. I'm not sure the local residents would buy it, or whether the farmer would sell it. At one point today there were thirteen children in the garden. Is this the way it's going to be, will they just turn up? I hope so.

Little Eversden was gorgeous. Rose has polished everything, the sky seemed clean – blue cold air that had been siphoned over snow somewhere. Simon suggested we pray for the England cricket team. Now that they've lost it we ought to. The radio this evening was about advertising the church. The panellists were pretty unanimous, thumbs down all round. The bigwig from the big London agency said the product is unsellable as it is, and certainly the limp nonsense churned out by Church House would confirm this. But what is the product? I don't think we should be advertising the churches, it's selling the wrapper not the sweets. We should leave them alone completely, take all the lines off the bottom of the posters. The best and worst advertisements for Christ have always been the people that believe in him. If you melt that down to a typeface and a visual the result is neither colourful nor mainstream. The advertising that the Churches Advertising Network produces always runs the risk of alienating those who pay for it. But I do feel passionate that the words spoken by Christ are all that's needed – they just need to be aired in a contemporary manner. They have been flattened and neutralised and have taken on the lustre of a tin of grapefruit segments. They either appear old-fashioned or are presented to us in a manner where the raconteur tries to convince you he has the solution to solve yours and the world's problems in one breath. The alarm bells go off in unison: if he's got the answer, why aren't we all living in peace and harmony, beaming with bliss? Christianity has too many salesmen and not enough practitioners. The strategy of electing lead bishops to talk on pre-set topics is fine, as long as we accept the fact that having adopted that strategy we are going to get canned in every corner; to subsequently moan at the media for toasting us really demonstrates we are not dealing with reality here. The picture of ourselves we see in the press is desperate, but the picture of humanity presented by the press is far worse: they sell us our weaknesses and by appealing to our weaknesses they will only make us weaker.

It was soft this morning, a lazy mist saturating the distance. The earthquake in Turkey was scratched on almost every front cover of the papers, unbelievable, inconceivable mayhem. How many people died dreaming the roof was falling in? It was strange to see rooms full of bread – there is too much, apparently – and then an awful rain soaking up the urban tents that had settled in parks and squares, children with mud in their eyes. The scientists say we can only survive, we can only breathe because the climate is unstable. Can you imagine the disbelief, the anger that God could do such a thing? I am angry. Yes, we could, we should build buildings that can cope; we don't because they cost too much, maybe that was the reason that has left so many orphans. Anger though will not heal anything, it crushes hope, bleeds any sense of peace. It's our choice, we choose our own response. The PCC meeting last night was actually enjoyable, as they should be. When I came to Haslingfield they were awful, utterly joyless. The meetings in Harlton were much better. It was as if people in Haslingfield had forgotten how to laugh. The rooms were mined, the tension tangled behind people's teeth. There was a real darkness in Haslingfield. I remember sitting there for the first two weeks or so once the voyeurs had been and gone, and we were left with who we were; it was heavy, oppressive.

We're in London for a night. There is a full moon and the planes come roaring in over the buildings; they are fantastic, shouting under the clouds. I left Sarah in the churchyard; she pushed her bike up the gravel path and we talked about God and how everything seems to have settled. We are so clumsy with love, we are complete amateurs really; it is too strong for most of us. We weep and become confused, our mind gets tangled up in our heart. Falling in love is a shocking thing. I'm amazed we still retell the fairy tale. It's there in every film, the same basic story: boy meets girl, man meets woman. How many of us have actually fallen in love, how many of us rode on our own wave, the wave that wanted to be in love? It is fierce when it happens, melts your hard soul, wreaks complete chaos; morality is no match for it. The trouble is the idea is so powerful, most of us love the idea, and that's what most of us believe in. Unless you have fallen in love it can only ever be an idea, a theory you believe in. There are no sacrifices made without it.

Would Christ have put his palms on the wood of the cross knowing the nails were coming? He was one of the few men who was able to make sense of love, the only man who could bear it without, it would seem, becoming deranged because of it. What did they say in Greek mythology, that human beings could not drink the gods' wine – it sent them mad? Christ said drink it, but if you do, be aware what it is you are tasting because having tasted it you can never be the same again. Most of us sip at it, we emerge from out of the shadows hardly daring, hardly believing, always questioning how much control we can afford to surrender; you see love is essentially anarchistic, will not obey boundaries, convention, order. It will always lead you to the truth about yourself.

The church has become too rigid – we have bought into this dreadful thing called success. The Sunday statistics are used as ballistics to prove how wrong we must be, how unsuccessful we are; we have consequently become obsessed with mission, with youth work; there is this suspicion we are not feeding the five thousand at all, we are feeding ourselves. We are losing the sense of God and godliness in our attempts to make God make sense. We need to stop blaming television or the media, or coke, or Eve, or alcohol, or sexual permissiveness, or greed. It's us, it's our fault we are where we are. Those who say the church is out of touch are absolutely right, thank God. It is perhaps more than anything else our ludicrous attempts to make ourselves more relevant, more hip, more acceptable definitely, more user-friendly, more accommodating, more theologically sound that have failed. What we really needed to be was more loving, more prayerful, more brave, more silent. We must stop avoiding the lions' den and start to try to get into it; we have been too quick to moralise and too slow to minister. I know I've clanged on about the structure of the church, but our current crisis cannot be solved by rejigging the management, by shorter working hours. We could have an army of committees dealing with this, dealing with that; none of it will make any difference at all other than change the wallpaper. Better PR is not the answer. I know that now. The problem has been our dependence on the structure and like fools, like the fool I have been, we assume that holds the key. It doesn't. We have become bereft of love, we have allowed process and the state and PCCs and faculties and banns and advertising and diocesan councils, boards of social responsibility, to take its place. The model that Christ left was one of love. We have depended on the system to exemplify God's love rather than depend on love to exemplify the system. When the public look at the Christian Church they don't see love – do you see love? They see ceremony, tradition, flower festivals, building projects, carol concerts, nativity plays. Where is our soul in all of this? We have foolishly believed it is all these things and more that are keeping the church going and still it declines. We devise ever grander schemes to woo the disaffected, to fill the theatre, really none of it is working. We have been handing out chocolate in the vain hope that this will satisfy some spiritual craving. I've spent too much time doing that. The model of love, that's all we have. We have been fools to think that it wasn't enough and even more foolish to presume we own it.

Well, we met for the millennium wall in Harlton. The idea is to build a wall where people's names can be inscribed rather than laying slabs of Swedish stone down on the ground for the grass to grow over. There were five or six bricks from the diocese. The stand-in archdeacon was aquiline; he listened attentively above the disagreements between the geese and the hens on the other side of the mesh fence that the bindweed had smothered. He suggested we make room for roses. I agree. They were the style guardians, the heritage hounds, there to sniff out the faintest hint of clashing colours. Their shoes were quintessentially English, the leather with punctured patterns, even laces. They knew how to mix concrete, to clean angels' wings, to glaze the glass, they were all excited about what was under the tower floor at Haslingfield which is going to be dug up in two weeks' time. The thing about manners is that they are catching; theirs were exquisite. It was a quiet soluble gentility that I hadn't felt for too many years; it was very, very, impressive indeed. None of them ever spoke over one another, they listened intently to what the other had to say. I just rolled up in the usual fashion, silly waistcoat, mouldy hat; it completely threw me.

Christ clearly was not interested in himself, he wasn't tied by his own ego at all. The entry into Jerusalem when he rode the donkey was an open invitation to be arrested. Here is the car thief driving down the high street at 10 mph in the nicked motor with the stereo blazing. The authorities obligingly stepped in. Christianity embodies this self-surrender; the presentation is blunt, but at its best it is a giving up of self, a giving up of ego to God. This is surely very threatening to a society such as ours, that practises the cult of reward. If you do away with eternity then actually nothing has any value at all. If you place yourself at the mercy of eternity – this is a brave and foolish thing to do – in the absence of any proof of any kind, it is far simpler to stay in the murky waters of mammon fumbling around for diamonds, getting high on Ferrari exhaust fumes, dressing up in logos, selling dreams, dream holidays, dream beer, dream clothes, dream bank accounts, dream yoghurt, dream kitchens. In England we have some of the best advertising in the world. Watch it, don't turn over – it is a parade of dreams, incredible really, there is nothing real at all in any of them. Like all dreams they may contain truth but not one of them is truth. Are we awake when we watch television or are we asleep? The problem is if we advertise we join the big dream; far from dealing with reality, we actually may well be giving it up.

The parish picnic was uneventful. We sat in the meadow, everyone brought food, there was a surplus of quiche. This was all planned to bring the Methodists and Anglicans up to each other's shoulders. It didn't really work – we needed a bloke with an accordion or a dancing nun or something other than plastic bowls full of chicken wings and ourselves. Sarah had made a lovely salad. We spoke about marriage this morning, how difficult it is; a letter arrived in the early hours berating the sermon on Sunday which was about this ancient institution. Your marriage as a priest becomes public property, so do your children. Happily they don't see that, but you can feel your relationship being walked over, talked over. You sacrifice privacy. People say things like I hope you and Jacs get to spend some time together, it's lovely really; you simply can't shut the shop though, it has to remain open.

The healing service seems to have echoed around the village. We're planning another one with a first service of the millennium in Haslingfield. We also agreed to share the reading of the Gospel from the New Year, so it won't just be muggins who reads it. I wish I could say I was excited about the millennium but I'm not really; I don't actually know what it means, I'm not sure what it is we are celebrating other than the obvious. There is still the suspicion that this is a private party; everyone keeps saying that Jesus is 2,000 years old and yet we are really no closer to knowing him, having lived with him all this time; each generation arrives with its own colours, its own agenda and obsessions and yet he has remained almost untouched. All the words, all the theology, all the rhetoric, he seems above it all. These are personal journeys really, trying to express something that words cannot contain. Wonderful really that the sacred language of speaking in tongues is nonsensical – its great meaning is in the speaker. We are always striving for humility, for money, for bricks, for survival, so very few of us just are.

The greatest gift churches can give us perhaps is that they are places that free us from success, failure, labels, television, radio, cars, posters, happy meals; places that embody the sense and the peace of God at work in us. Human doing has bled human being, it has taken up so much precious time. Time to explore your soul, the greatest landscape of all.

Small Boat, Big Sea

Alan Freeman was on television late last night, cast as God. He sat there in billowing dry ice behind a couple of record decks, while Marianne Faithful wandered across the clouds dispensing truth in song. English priests, when we are scripted in comedy ink might as well have been tattooed by it. The characters are frighteningly true, we are largely Moles of *Wind in the Willows* or dreadful laminations of TV psychotherapists. We are morning television material, that's about as serious as it gets: on the couch with Reverend Smith. All this represents a failure of staggering proportions by those charged with religious programming – about as inspiring as another Cliff Richard single. The football's still very hit and miss, my mind runs faster than my legs and the own goal that I scored definitely had more skill in it than the two that somehow managed to nutmeg the goalie.

It's all picking up again. The summer has been wonderful. We assume that a calling is something that happens, something priests experience; then they respond, and then once they respond the stardust stops. It doesn't. The experience of God, the Holy Spirit, isn't something that becomes worn and predictable. The calling, for all of us, continues all the time; we just call it something else, that's all, a relationship with God, a prayer life, an abiding sense of the Holy Spirit. I'm not sure it's something we will ever get used to – as time goes on we perhaps become less responsive, we measure love in hours and minutes spent, in our own capacity to give rather than what we have been given. It doesn't wane, we do. Given the practical workload that's understandable, I think, and in that sense we should be doing less not more.

As a way of life it has surpassed all my expectations. I am constantly moved by people's extraordinary courage when faced with what appears to be tragedy, constantly calmed by the sense and calling of God in others, always humbled by the generosity and grace of my colleagues and all those in the parishes who have patiently endured my mistakes and inexperience. To a large extent it is others that make you what you are. I do not share the popular view that the church is dying, that Christianity has had its day; the church is shedding a skin, that's all. Everyone seems hypnotised by the cracks they can see – they should look deeper. The way in which we express Christian faith in the context of our culture undoubtedly needs change, but that shouldn't be interpreted as Christianity coming to an end. No, it is simply coming to a new beginning and there have been several of those within the last millennium. I have also learned that when we eat the bread, drink the wine, we become part of the suffering, we accept a calling of suffering. 'This is my body, broken for you,' 'This is my blood, shed for you.' So much of what we plan is to avoid this suffering, to alleviate suffering, but as priests we are also called to suffer. That may seem completely perverse, ringing in the prevailing wind, and indeed runs against the models of success that we are continually tempted with, but it is there, deep in the heart of life. Despite my genuinely dreadful behaviour I can only say that the God that I experience is one of infinite patience and love and it is always my own lack of courage to face up to that, to accept it for what it is, that creates the tensions that lead to loneliness. This inner loneliness, which is ultimately a denial of soul, is the greatest disease of our age. It is the sub-plot for so much. It is the grace of God that ultimately saves us all.

The greengages have fallen from the trees – they lie open on the soil. The wasps move slowly, stoned on the fermenting juice. The first of the Michaelmas daisies are beginning to flower, a cross between purple and blue – the feathered petals have yellow centres. There are two Red Admirals in the garden dipping in and out of sunlight and the house martins are gathering in the sky ready to go back to Africa. These things are extraordinary in themselves, so are you. There is a wonderful line on the roof of the Synod Chamber in London. It reads, 'Thy holy light is passing wonderful.' It is; in it we are blessed beyond our imagining. It's September.

Printed in Great Britain
by Amazon